The American History Series

SERIES EDITORS
John Hope Franklin, *Duke University*
A. S. Eisenstadt, *Brooklyn College*

D. Clayton James
Anne Sharp Wells
VIRGINIA MILITARY INSTITUTE

America and the Great War

1914–1920

HARLAN DAVIDSON, INC.
WHEELING, ILLINOIS 60090-6000

Visit us on the World Wide Web at www.harlandavidson.com.

Library of Congress Cataloging-in-Publication Data

James, D. Clayton
    America and the Great War, 1914–1920 / D. Clayton James, Anne Sharp Wells.
        p. cm. — (The American history series)
    Includes bibliographical references and index.
    ISBN 978-0-88295-944-3
    1. World War, 1914–1918 — United States. 2. World War, 1914–1918 — Social aspects — United States. 3. United States — Politics and government — 1913–1921. I. Wells, Anne Sharp. II. Title. III. Series: American history series (Wheeling, Ill.)
D570.J36   1998
940.3'73 — dc21   97-40739
                                           CIP

Cover photograph: "Over the Top." U.S. Army Signal Corps photo. Reproduced courtesy of George C. Marshall Research Library, Lexington, Virginia.

Manufactured in the United States of America
07 2 MG

FOREWORD

Every generation writes its own history for the reason that it sees the past in the foreshortened perspective of its own experience. This has surely been true of the writing of American history. The practical aim of our historiography is to give us a more informed sense of where we are going by helping us understand the road we took in getting where we are. As the nature and dimensions of American life are changing, so too are the themes of our historical writing. Today's scholars are hard at work reconsidering every major aspect of the nation's past: its politics, diplomacy, economy, society, recreation, mores and values, as well as status, ethnic, race, sexual, and family relations. The lists of series titles that appear on the inside covers of this book will show at once that our historians are ever broadening the range of their studies.

The aim of this series is to offer our readers a survey of what today's historians are saying about the central themes and aspects of the American past. To do this, we have invited to write for the series only scholars who have made notable contributions to the respective fields in which they are working. Drawing on primary and secondary materials, each volume presents a factual and narrative account of its particular subject, one that affords readers a basis for perceiving its larger dimensions and importance. Conscious that readers respond to the closeness and immediacy of a subject, each of our authors seeks to restore the past as an actual present, to revive it as a living reality. The individuals and groups who figure in the pages of our books appear as real people who once were looking for survival and fulfillment. Aware that historical subjects are often matters of controversy, our authors present their own findings and conclusions. Each volume closes with an extensive critical essay on the writings of the major authorities on its particular theme.

The books in this series are primarily designed for use in both basic and advanced courses in American history, on the undergraduate and graduate levels. Such a series has a particular value these days, when the format of American history courses is being altered to accommodate a greater diversity of reading materials. The series offers a number of distinct advantages. It extends the dimensions of regular course work. It makes clear that the study of our past is, more than the student might otherwise understand, at once complex, profound, and absorbing. It presents that past as a subject of continuing interest and fresh investigation.

For these reasons the series strongly invites an interest that far exceeds the walls of academe. The work of experts in their respective fields, it puts at the disposal of all readers the rich findings of historical inquiry, an invitation to join, in major fields of research, those who are pondering anew the central themes and aspects of our past.

And, going beyond the confines of the classroom, it reminds the general reader no less than the university student that in each successive generation of the ever-changing American adventure, from its very start until our own day, men and women and children were facing their daily problems and attempting, as we are now, to live their lives and to make their way.

John Hope Franklin
A. S. Eisenstadt

CONTENTS

ACKNOWLEDGMENTS

This study is largely a distillation of the findings of many historians who have explored the various aspects of America's involvement in the First World War and its immediate aftermath. We are grateful also to the staff members who assisted us in the National Archives, Washington, D.C.; and the staffs of the following institutions in Lexington, Virginia: the Preston Library of the Virginia Military Institute, the Leyburn Library of Washington and Lee University, and the George C. Marshall Research Library. Andrew Davidson, our editor at Harlan Davidson, Inc., gave indispensable assistance to this project, as did John Hope Franklin and A. S. Eisenstadt, editors of the American History Series. Strong logistical support was provided by the Virginia Military Institute Foundation and administration. As with our previous books, Erlene James was invaluable at every stage from research to proofreading.

D. Clayton James
Anne Sharp Wells

May 1997

To the J. T. Spencers
and the D. M. Joneses

CHAPTER ONE

The Tangled Paths to Horror in Europe

The American people traditionally have reacted with surprise when large wars begin overseas, even those ultimately involving the United States. Thus it was in late June 1914 when a Serb nationalist in Sarajevo assassinated the visiting heir to the Austrian throne. Why this seemingly minor incident in Bosnia precipitated a massive European conflict within five weeks mystified most citizens of the United States, where the average adult knew little about the situation in Europe. Actually, during the previous two decades Europe had divided into two camps, each armed to the teeth, and their maneuverings in the Balkans and Morocco had almost ignited widespread warfare several times.

Partly because of a complicated system of prewar alliances, the Sarajevo shooting soon escalated into widespread war. Furious, Austria-Hungary issued an ultimatum to Serbia and declared war on July 28, after Serbia protested some of its demands. Consequently, Russia, a Serbian ally, mobilized its forces and ignored German warnings to cease. After Germany's subsequent declaration of war against Russia on August 1, France, as Russia's ally, ordered its armies to mobilize. Announcing its decision to go to war with France on August 3, Germany immediately moved to attack French forces by marching through neutral Belgium. Due to its defense pact with Belgium, Great Britain declared war on Germany on August 4. A number of other war declarations followed.

The hostilities lasted from 1914 until November 1918, when the last armistice was signed. At the start of the war, the major Allied powers were Britain, France, and Russia, soon joined by Japan and later by Italy. Among the other Allies were Belgium, Greece, Montenegro, Portugal, Rumania, Serbia, and members of the British Empire—Australia, Canada, India, South Africa, and New Zealand. Opposing them were the Central powers of Germany and Austria-Hungary, with Turkey (the Ottoman Empire) and Bulgaria added later.

In western Europe, most of the fighting took place in France, as German armies met British, Belgian, and French (and later American) forces on the Western Front. During much of the same period, Germany also faced Russian soldiers on the Eastern Front, until the horrendous casualties helped to provoke the Russian revolution and Russia's exit from the war in late 1917. Turkey fought against Russia in the Caucasus and Persia, while battling British forces in Mesopotamia, Egypt, and the Dardanelles, site of the failed British invasion at Gallipoli. The forces of Austria-Hungary and Italy clashed near the border northwest of Trieste. Japan's primary participation in the war was its seizure of German territories in Asia and the Pacific. In Africa and elsewhere, the belligerents contested colonial possessions.

When war began on the European continent, Americans could not imagine its scope and human cost, but they condemned its outbreak. To former President William Howard Taft, the war was "a cataclysm," "a retrograde step in Christian civilization," and "a disaster to mankind." Senator John Sharp Williams felt "mad all over" as well as "sick and irritable" at the start of this "senseless war." The *New York Times* had harsh words for all involved: "The European nations have reverted to the condition of savage tribes roaming in the forest and falling upon each other in a fury of carnage to achieve the ambitious designs of chieftains clad in skin and drunk on mead." One newspaper editor summed up the views of many: "We have never appreciated so keenly as now the foresight exercised by our forefathers in emigrating from Europe."

In 1914, nearly one-third of the population of the United States was foreign born or the children of immigrants. Initially, they tended to sympathize with the countries from which their families came, while opposing any formal involvement in the war by the United States. The majority of Americans generally favored Great Britain and France and blamed Germany for starting the hostilities. Those with British backgrounds leaned most strongly toward the nation that had created much of their literature, language, governmental forms, and legal codes. And ever since the Revolutionary War, the people of the United States had nourished a fond feeling toward the French, who had helped Americans gain independence while trying to thwart Britain.

German Americans and Irish Americans constituted two of the most numerous and influential of the non-English groups in America. Many German Americans lived in close-knit communities where they retained German customs and language in both social and commercial settings. In Texas alone, where German Americans made up a small percentage of the population, twenty-four newspapers were published in German. When war broke out, many German Americans immediately defended Germany's cause against its adversaries. In light of Ireland's continuing struggle for freedom from Britain, Irish Americans were unenthusiastic about helping the British, but generally preferred the Allies to the Central powers. Most Americans, whatever their backgrounds, considered the war to be a European affair and envisioned no American participation in it.

As his wife lay dying in the White House in early August, President Woodrow Wilson officially proclaimed the neutrality of the United States. Two weeks later he publicly called on the entire citizenry to be "impartial in thought as well as in action." While recognizing that "the people of the United States are drawn . . . chiefly from the nations now at war," the president urged Americans to avoid partisanship and to perform "our duty as the one great nation at peace." In Wilson's view, the World War stemmed from rampant imperialism, covert alliance terms, unjustifiable arms rivalries, and failures in moral leadership by the European nations. He hoped that the United States would "play a part of impartial mediation" in resolving the conflict.

Wilson's decisions on international matters often appeared idealistic, but actually combined moral diplomacy and practicality. In his deepest convictions he opposed the old world order and wanted the leading nations to embrace a more liberal and less imperialistic approach to international politics. In trying to accomplish this, however, he distanced himself from many of his own liberal supporters. Highly principled and often highly partisan, Wilson at times encountered difficulties in steering a consistent course.

Although he pledged to keep the United States neutral, the president's ties were closer to the Allies than to the Central powers. A former professor and president of Princeton University, Wilson was a noted scholar of British government and history. Moreover, his major advisers on the belligerents were pro-British: Edward M. House, his chief confidant and principal liaison with key European statesmen; and Robert Lansing, his main foreign-policy adviser.

When the war began, Wilson's secretary of state was William Jennings Bryan, who had been appointed because of his strong base in the Democratic party and his support of Wilson's presidential candidacy in 1912. The two men were not close. Bryan, a longtime popular crusader, spent time on the lecture circuit away from Washington and was ridiculed by foreign diplomats for serving grape juice instead of alcohol at official functions. Wilson often bypassed Bryan by acting as his own secretary of state or by sending House on diplomatic missions, but the president did agree with his secretary on the importance of American neutrality, at least in the beginning. The following year Bryan resigned over presidential actions he considered biased against Germany and likely to lead to war.

Much closer to the president was "Colonel" House, a wealthy Texan with widespread financial interests in cotton and banking. He was also experienced and influential in Democratic politics at the state and national levels. House preferred to operate and exercise his power behind the scenes, leading one senator to say, "He can walk on dead leaves and make no more noise than a tiger." Wilson looked to him for friendship and counsel, especially following the death of his first wife, Ellen Axson Wilson. In numerous missions to Paris, London, and Berlin from 1914 to 1916, House was invaluable in representing the president; he later served ably on the Allied Supreme War Council, the armistice commission, and the American delegation to the peace conference. House usually based his advice to the president on common sense rather than on extensive knowledge of European affairs and leaders.

It was at House's urging that Wilson shifted Lansing from the State Department's counselor position to succeed Bryan as secretary of state in 1915. Lansing, a reserved New Yorker with impeccable manners, had earned a reputation as a distinguished international attorney prior to joining the government. His judgments throughout the war were influenced strongly by his strains of legalism, sometimes too much so. Lansing was one of the first of Wilson's inner circle to become convinced that the United States eventually would have to enter the war on the Allied side to protect neutral rights and basic American economic and security interests.

Another pro-British member of the administration was Walter Hines Page, ambassador to the Court of St. James. Page championed the British position so strongly that the president discounted his advice, considering him "too much affected by the English" perspective. The ambassador, nevertheless, retained his position throughout the war, since Wilson found it "rather useful to have him give us the English view of things so straight." Eventually, however, the president stopped reading Page's messages altogether.

For more than two and one-half years of the war, the United States remained officially neutral. Throughout this period the Allies and the Central powers alternately ignored, courted, or threatened the American position. Although Wilson ultimately became convinced that a German triumph would pose a serious menace to U.S. security, as well as to the heritage of Western civilization, he continued to avoid American intervention in the conflict. The president remained confident that he could successfully mediate between the warring camps and end the horrors that were occurring around the world.

Bloodbaths But No Decision

The conflict of 1914–1918 was justifiably known as "The Great War" or "The World War." An unprecedented number of belligerent nations fought engagements large and small on three continents, six seas, and at least two oceans. The totals of people affected by the war were staggering: over 65 million military personnel were engaged, with 8 million killed in combat and more than 21 million wounded. The losses among civilians were even higher. Additionally, countless others, both uniformed and civilian, died from diseases made deadlier by war conditions, especially the huge influenza-pneumonia epidemics that spread rapidly in 1918. The war cost more than $281 billion in military expenses and damage to civilian property.

The ground operations, in terms of personnel losses, were the costliest in military annals up to that time. One traditional explanation for the huge casualties is that military technology had outpaced tactical doctrine. In the Russo-Japanese War of 1904–1905, military observers had glimpsed much-improved ordnance and new weapons but had not yet recognized their significance. By 1914, massed concentrations of artillery and machine-gun fire had shifted the advantage in battle from the attacker to the defender. One authority attributed the losses not to doctrine but "to inefficiency, inexperience, and the sheer organizational problems of combining fire and movement on the requisite scale." Just as the world's large cities would become too populous and complicated for effective control, so the World War's massive demonstration of manpower and firepower grew beyond the management ability of its commanders. Until a fresh military strategy or diplomatic solution could be found, uncoordinated, indecisive operations continued.

In August 1914, German troops marched through Belgium on their path to France, where British and French forces brought the advance to a halt with huge casualties on both sides. To defend against the deadly firepower, soldiers took up the spade and dug in. By October a line of trenches extended from the English Channel south to the Swiss border, nearly 500 miles. For more than two years, the frontline of the Western Front remained static, as each side launched costly frontal assaults while failing to move forward more than a few miles in any direction.

Trench warfare came to symbolize the Western Front to both Europeans and Americans. Between the opposing trenches were several hundred yards of bleak territory known as "no man's land," which contained barbed wire, unexploded munitions, shell holes, weeds, and debris. In the trenches the troops shared their unhealthy muddy quarters with rats and lice, as well as the bodies of dead comrades. They had no place to lie down and constantly contended with snipers and incessant artillery fire, commonly resulting in the psychological condition called shell shock. When troops were ordered out of the trenches to charge across no man's land toward enemy positions, machine gunfire stopped them in large numbers; those who survived the spray of bullets then fought in close combat with bayonets, knives, and grenades.

Another horror of this war was poison gas, introduced by the Germans and later used by all parties. Its effectiveness was limited by the need to rely on favorable wind conditions to control its direction. Although relatively few people actually died from the gases, many were seriously injured by them. The most hazardous was mustard gas, which blistered exposed skin, caused temporary blindness, and burned the linings of the throat and lungs. To defend against the clouds of gas, British soldiers initially tried to protect their faces with cloths soaked in urine. Later the British, French, and Germans developed effective gas masks, which were worn by both men and horses near the front.

The magnitude of the killing and maiming was mind boggling. In the first Marne battle in northern France in September 1914, the British, French, and German armies suffered over a half million casualties, with an additional 1.3 million killed and wounded in the two months that followed. The horrific losses continued on the Western Front and in other parts of the world as well. Particularly deadly were the Caporetto-Isonzo campaign in northern Italy (432,000 casualties) and the Gallipoli assault in Turkey

(502,000 casualties). The largest human losses suffered by one nation occurred on the Eastern Front, where Russian casualties of 7 million troops and 2 million civilians contributed to the coming revolution. In turn the Russians inflicted monstrous losses on the German war machine, which never fully recovered.

One campaign especially illustrative of the costly yet indecisive warfare of the Western Front was the First Battle of the Somme, which lasted from June to November 1916. In an offensive coordinated with the French, the British bombarded German positions with artillery for several days before launching an attack with infantry. British commanders believed their intense shelling had destroyed enemy defenses and would permit their troops to walk across open ground to the German positions. The British forces included volunteers from all levels of society, who often served in groups from the same villages, clubs, and schools. They were inexperienced but enthusiastic, with several platoons kicking footballs as they left the trenches and set out across no man's land on July 1. Far from being devastated by the prior shelling, German forces mowed down the British troops with machine guns. In the first hour the British lost nearly 30,000 men, wiping out the contingents of entire neighborhoods. The day's grisly casualty toll was 60,000, with one-third of those men dying. In spite of the catastrophic first day, the campaign continued for six months and cost both sides 1.3 million casualties. At the end of the carnage, the Allies had gained only seven miles of territory.

By late 1916, the combatants on the Western Front had largely given up hope of significant territorial conquests or quick annihilation of large enemy forces. In desperation the commanders on both sides turned to fighting a war of attrition, or forcing the enemy to expend soldiers steadily in indecisive but virtually unremitting combat. The use of field artillery, which accounted for most infantry deaths, changed intended battles of movement into terrible killing grounds. Field Marshal Douglas Haig, head of the British Expeditionary Force, reported to his London superiors that November: "In another six weeks the enemy should be hard put to it to find men. . . . The maintenance of a steady offensive pressure will result eventually in his complete overthrow." The top British,

French, and German commanders on the Western Front all viewed the great losses of the Somme operations as a supreme test of the fitness of both their armies and their nations to survive by enduring huge human sacrifices, though costing their countries the cream of a generation of young manhood. Surely, such military thinking was desperate, but it was a time of despair for most government leaders in the capitals of all the warring powers.

While the human suffering of the ground war appalled Americans, the war at sea directly threatened to involve the United States in the conflict. In the early stages of hostilities, neither side seriously viewed the United States as a potential force that could end the war. Until early 1917 the main warring powers treated the United States with ambivalence, aggravating the giant country with violations of its neutral rights yet assiduously trying to win over American public opinion. The venue for many of the clashes was the sea.

Britain was brazen in its disregard of Wilson's sentiments on neutrality. Its Royal Navy controlled the surface waters throughout the war and effectively blockaded Germany, declaring the North Sea to be a war zone and sowing it with mines. Through its naval power the British restricted American mail delivery, travel, and shipping with both enemy and neutral countries. In addition to banning arms and items clearly related to the conduct of war, the British embargoed materials such as cotton and tobacco. They declared foodstuffs to be contraband and forcibly searched American vessels to impose their edicts. As a further insult, the British government blacklisted American firms it accused of conducting business with the enemy. The United States repeatedly protested the violations of its neutral rights, at times so vehemently that Ambassador Page warned that relations with Britain were being damaged. British leaders basically ignored American objections and took for granted Wilson's sympathy toward the Allies. This attitude galled the White House but was in fact a largely accurate appraisal.

American honor, rights, and property were threatened by British actions, but American lives were menaced by German submarines. As Britain's blockade of Germany tightened and its own ability to receive supplies remained undisturbed, the Germans increasingly turned to the use of underseas boats (U-boats) to counter the British advantage. Berlin defined as a war zone the waters around the United Kingdom, including the English Channel and the French coast. Within this zone Germany unleashed its large submarine fleet against not only vessels of the Allied navies but also noncombatant Allied ships.

On May 7, 1915, a German U-boat near the Irish coast torpedoed and sank the British passenger ship *Lusitania,* which was traveling from the United States to Britain. On the day the luxury liner, called "Queen of the Seas," left New York, American newspapers carried a German warning that "travellers sailing in the war zone on ships of Great Britain or her allies do so at their own risk." Still, Americans were shocked when the *Lusitania* sank, killing 1,200 in all, including 128 Americans and many infants.

American newspapers vehemently condemned the sinking of the passenger ship, labeling it "slaughter," "plain and unqualified piracy," "wholesale murder," and a "crime against civilization." One editor charged that "there is no shadow of excuse for it in military necessity." Another wrote that "Germany surely must have gone mad" in its "reckless disregard of the opinions of the world in general and this country in particular." Several newspapers asserted the right of neutral Americans to travel on any ships they chose without risking their lives. Adding to the outrage were justifications by German representatives that anyone who ignored the German warning about travel could "commit suicide if he wants to." Other Germans defended the sinking on the grounds that the *Lusitania* carried contraband cargo.

The president reacted cautiously at first, telling one audience that America should set "a special example" to the world. He continued: "There is such a thing as a nation being so right that it does not need to convince others by force that it is right. . . . There is such a thing as a man being too proud to fight." Wilson then sent two notes to Germany, protesting the sinking and demanding protection of American lives in the future. The second and stronger note exposed a split in the administration and resulted in the resignation of Secretary of State Bryan, who claimed that the United States was not behaving impartially toward Germany. He defended the German "right to prevent contraband going to the Allies" and stated that "a ship carrying contraband should not rely upon passengers to protect her from attack—it would be like putting women and children in front of an army." Rejecting attempts to persuade him to remain in office to protect the unity of the administration, Bryan repeated his desire for peace and explained, "I believe that I can do more on the outside to prevent war than I can on the inside." After resigning, on June 9, Bryan worked with the pacifist movement.

Other advisers to the president disagreed with Bryan's view of the *Lusitania* matter. House asserted, "We can no longer remain neutral." Page wrote that "Notes don't hurt Germans" and concluded that the United States would have to enter the war to "put down the wild beast now loose in the world." Lansing, who formally was appointed as Bryan's successor on June 23, told House: "In no event should we take a course that would seriously damage our friendly relations with Great Britain, France, or Russia, for, as you say, our friendship with Germany is a thing of the past."

American negotiations with Germany proceeded slowly, while U-boats continued to target Allied ships and cause American casualties. The following spring the Germans torpedoed the French ship *Sussex,* which carried several Americans. This time Wilson publicly threatened to break diplomatic relations with Germany, which responded by temporarily ending its policy of unrestricted submarine warfare. German frustration over the naval situation remained.

Germany's use of submarines provided the British with one of their best propaganda tools to portray the Germans as "a dastardly lot descended from ancient warmongering barbarians." The Allies claimed that the German submariners violated rules of international law, namely, that the enemy challenger must prove that a noncombatant ship carried contraband before destroying the vessel and must then provide for the safety of the passengers and crew of the targeted ship. Of course, submarines that surfaced for such purposes would have done so at great risk since they were highly vulnerable when not submerged; moreover, they were hardly equipped to care for a large number of additional persons. Regardless, most Americans agreed that the use of submarines, exploited mainly by the Germans, was a barbaric infraction of the human principles that were supposed to govern the conduct of war among civilized peoples.

Early in the war the British government mobilized skilled propagandists to promote the Allied cause in the United States. Well-known writers such as Rudyard Kipling, Thomas Hardy, Arthur Conan Doyle, and John Masefield wrote pro-Allied articles that were offered for publication to American journals and newspapers. Throughout the United States, the British sponsored speaking tours and organized traveling exhibits of Allied war posters, which were extremely effective at disseminating information and influencing the public in an era lacking radio or TV broadcasts. The propagandists also encouraged a number of American journalists, professors, ministers, and others to advance Allied positions. One early advocate was Richard Harding Davis, an American reporter who had witnessed the German invasion of Belgium and wrote soon afterward: "Were the conflict in Europe a fair fight, the duty of every American would be to keep on the side-lines and preserve an open mind. But it is not a fair fight." He accused Germany of "defying the rules of war and the rules of humanity" and concluded: "When a mad dog runs amuck in a village it is the duty of every farmer to get his gun and destroy it, not to lock himself indoors and toward the dog and the men who face him preserve a neutral mind."

The Allies' attempts to demonize their enemies were facilitated by clumsy German actions, such as Chancellor Theobald von Bethmann Hollweg's dismissal of Belgian neutrality as merely "a scrap of paper." Propagandists called Germany's invasion "the rape of Belgium" and attributed monstrous atrocities to the German soldiers. Much of the American populace naively accepted the exaggerated accounts, many of which were refuted after the war. In the most frequently repeated versions, Germans were accused of dealing with Belgians by spearing babies with bayonets, cutting off women's breasts, crucifying soldiers who resisted, and carrying out widespread raping and looting. Appearing on numerous posters and cartoons throughout the world was the image of the inhuman, helmeted German soldier carrying a bayonet dripping with blood. Propaganda stories later in the war described German factories that supposedly manufactured soap and fertilizer from the bodies of dead German soldiers.

The Allied propaganda campaign also benefited from episodes of espionage and sabotage committed by German and Austrian agents in the United States. Attempting to prevent the flow of American supplies to the Allies, they bombed numerous factories, depots, and bridges while bungling other attempts. More annoying than substantial, their actions eventually provoked the Wilson administration into ousting a number of German and Austrian diplomats stationed across America. These episodes contributed to American hostility toward the Central powers.

In comparison to the Allies, German attempts at propaganda in America were lamentable. The arguments that reached Americans, largely through the German-American press, were often crude translations from German into English that appeared legalistic, arrogant, or simply too dull to interest most citizens. Some of the American representatives of the Central powers were professors who tended to sound bombastic instead of persuasive. The public largely rejected their defense of Germany's actions and their accusations that the British and French committed atrocities in Europe. Early in the war the British severely handicapped the German campaign to influence U.S. public opinion by cutting the cable service from Germany to America. For the rest of the conflict Britain controlled the Atlantic cable traffic to the United States, enabling its propaganda agencies to deliver selectively and to distort freely the most up-to-date news of the war, while German communications were extremely limited.

As the Allies prevailed in the contest to win American sympathy during the period of U.S. neutrality, they also strengthened their economic ties with the United States in a number of ways. The Royal Navy's surface dominance of the Atlantic prevented German ships from reaching American ports and within a year of the war's start had virtually ended trade between the Central powers and the United States. In contrast, the value of arms and ammunition shipments from the United States to the Allies soared dramatically, from $14.7 million in August 1915 to $74.9 million in August 1916, with the annual value of American munitions exports rising to almost $1.3 billion in 1916. An influential German commentator reflected his government's consternation when he exclaimed: "Germany finds herself in the position of a warrior, hemmed in on all sides. . . . Every time the warrior succeeds in disarming the foe most harmful to him . . . a so-called neutral comes running from behind and places a new weapon in the hand of the defeated foe."

Besides the burgeoning armament dealings with the Allies between 1914 and 1916, American exporters supplied increasing quantities of wheat, corn, processed foods, factory and farm machinery, pharmaceuticals, and countless other products that were needed by both military forces and civilian populations. The food relief from the United States was especially timely for England on several occasions when some of its basic food stocks had dropped to within six weeks of depletion.

During the period of neutrality, American banks made large loans to the Allies. Early in the war, Bryan expressed the fear of many that such loans would "make it all the more difficult for us to maintain neutrality," because "the powerful financial interests that would be connected with these loans would be tempted to use their influence through the newspapers" to affect the outcome of the war. In spite of misgivings, the Wilson administration eventually approved advances to the Allies that totaled over $10 billion by the end of the conflict. These loans boosted the recession-stricken American economy in 1915 and 1916 because the Allies mainly used them to make purchases in the United States. The boom eliminated fears of depression and brought prosperity to much of the country's manufacturing, commercial, agricultural, and shipping enterprises. In addition, it dramatically changed the global trade position of the United States from a long-time debtor to the world's foremost creditor, if a selective one. Also linking the United States more closely to the Allies in this period, American investors demonstrated clearly their leanings among the belligerents by purchasing $2.3 billion in British and French bonds in contrast to only $20 million in German bonds.

During the postwar years when isolationist sentiments swept the nation, a Senate investigation charged that American arms trafficking and bankers' profiteering had led to the United States' needless entry into the Great War. Actually, while the president favored the heavy investment in the Allied cause and approved of the boosting of domestic prosperity, these factors did not determine his involvement in the war. Instead, he shared the desire of most of his countrymen to keep Americans out of the horrors of European trenches.

A Time of Many Excitements

Alexis de Tocqueville, the perceptive Frenchman who visited the United States in the early 1830s, compared its society to Mississippi River steamboats, which produced much smoke and noise and whose boilers exploded with disturbing frequency. Had de Tocqueville stayed longer, he would have found that America goes through cycles of excitement and calm, reform and reaction.

The era of the Wilson presidency, 1913–1921, was one of excitement and reform both in domestic affairs, with the progressive movement reaching its zenith, and in foreign relations, with multiple interventions and crusades in Europe, Latin America, and East Asia. At home and abroad Americans displayed a much heightened interest in reforming their own society and those of other nations through such principles as honor, justice, human rights, self-determination of all peoples, and democracy. Whatever the terms meant—and they differed among reformers at different levels—the democratic impulse may have been the most broad-based and amorphous among them, for progressives were excited about political, economic, and social democracy—and not just for America. Still, the stirrings of the progressive era produced a host of significant, lasting domestic changes, though the results of the American interventions in the name of reforming other countries were more ephemeral and surely more dangerous.

During the age of progressivism, which ranged roughly from 1890 to 1920, the reformist spirit was manifest most prominently in Protestant, middle-class urbanites who had grown up in the heyday of the Robber Barons, Social Darwinism, and Victorian morality. "Having lost the literal faith of their ancestors," says a noted scholar of the movement, "progressive leaders still wanted religious values to dominate political and economic life; they wanted better and fairer competition; and they wanted every citizen to participate." They seldom agreed, however, on the specifics of how "to remoralize society." On the local level, they elected enlightened mayors and battled reactionary urban political machines. State-level progressives accomplished the direct election of United States senators and state judges; plebiscites to initiate legislation and recall state officials; and fairer tax, welfare, and work laws. Wilson's immediate presidential predecessors, Theodore Roosevelt and Taft, had set a commendable pace in pursuing progressive goals on the national scale, such as better regulation of railroads and conservation of public lands.

When he moved to the White House in 1913, Wilson eagerly anticipated leading the country to even greater progressive achievements in domestic affairs, telling a friend, "It would be the irony of fate if my administration had to deal chiefly with foreign affairs." Although much of his energy was indeed consumed with crises abroad, he still contributed to domestic reforms such as tariff reduction, more effective antitrust legislation, federal funding of agriculture and education, revision of the national tax laws, and establishment of the Federal Reserve system. Wilson gave new meaning to the international dimension of progressivism as he took the nation into the World War and tried in vain to make America a charter member of the League of Nations. If progressivism was essentially a religious fervor, he and Roosevelt were its leading missionaries on the international scene during their White House years.

While focusing on domestic affairs and maintaining a policy of neutrality in Europe, the president challenged Japan's growing aggressiveness and intervened militarily in Latin America. The militarist course followed by Japan had concerned American presidents for twenty years. In 1914 Japan entered the war on the side of the Allies and immediately targeted Germany's holdings in China and the Pacific. Violating Chinese sovereignty and outraging Berlin's leaders, Japan sent its troops into the mineral-rich Shantung Peninsula of North China that November and quickly took over Germany's sphere of influence there, capturing mines, railways, and the big Tsingtao naval base. In the West Pacific, meanwhile, other Japanese forces took the Marshall, Caroline, and Mariana archipelagos, which had been German colonies.

Wilson reacted most strongly to Japan's ultimatum in 1915 to revolution-paralyzed China. If China had agreed to all the demands, it would have become a Japanese protectorate. Risking a potentially dangerous confrontation with Japan, the State Department notified Tokyo that the United States government "could not regard with indifference the assumption of political, military, or economic domination over China by a foreign power." Preoccupied with the war in Europe, the Allied powers did not try to curb Japan's machinations in Asia, making ineffective Wilson's stratagem to alter Tokyo's course by denunciation alone. Japan compelled China to grant all the demands except the ones most egregious to Wilson, which were quietly dropped, and the president discreetly backed away from a confrontation. His options were limited: The American-owned Philippine Islands were vulnerable if Japan decided to move southward, and the United States lacked forces sufficient to deter Japan from that course of action. Wilson remained wary of Japanese expansionism and viewed Japan's growing relationship with Mexico as a grave concern.

As president, Wilson continued to intervene in Latin America, as had Roosevelt and Taft. In 1915 and 1916 he sent American troops and bankers into Haiti and the Dominican Republic to establish political order and economic stability. He forced Nicaragua to lease to the United States a naval base site and two offshore islands, as well as rights to an isthmus canal route. These countries would remain virtual American protectorates until the 1930s. Also, by virtue of the Platt Amendment of 1901, the Wilson administration continued to exercise control over Cuba's foreign relations and public finances, besides further strengthening the American naval station at Guantanamo Bay on the island's southeast coast. Washington also retained its right to intervene in Cuba to preserve law, order, and "independence."

After the outbreak of the World War, growing rumors of German intentions to move into Central America and the Caribbean led to the construction of American bases in Puerto Rico and the Panama Canal Zone. With the opening of the canal in 1914, its security soon became the linchpin of American strategy in the region and the rationale for reinforcements ashore and at sea. In 1916 the United States granted limited territorial status to Puerto Rico and the following year added its last colony, purchasing the western part of the Virgin Islands from Denmark.

The American relationship with Mexico received much attention from Wilson. Just as he began his presidency in early 1913, the commander of the Mexican Army, General Victoriano Huerta, seized control in Mexico and had its liberal, reformist president assassinated. Most nations recognized the Huerta regime despite its reactionary, militaristic nature, but Wilson refused. He expressed shock at the general's violent ascent to power and condemned "those who seek to seize the power of government to advance their own personal interests or ambition." He instituted an arms embargo against the Huerta government but left the door open for armament shipments to the dissident proconstitutionalist forces of Venustiano Carranza, which were on the rise in the countryside. However, even Carranza soon denounced Wilson and American interference in Mexican affairs—a popular move in gaining wide support among his people.

Frustrated with the Mexican morass, Wilson in April 1914 used a minor incident at the Mexican port of Tampico as "an affair of honor" that would give him the justification for armed intervention. After Huerta's soldiers temporarily seized a few American sailors, the United States demanded that Mexico apologize with a twenty-gun salute to the American flag. When Huerta boldly demanded a comparable salute to the Mexican flag by the Americans, Wilson called upon Congress to approve force to obtain "redress of grievances."

By the time Congress granted the president's request, he already had ordered the seizure of Veracruz, which was accomplished after a naval bombardment of the city and an assault by

Marines. Critics in the United States, Latin America, and Europe branded the capture of Veracruz a reckless risk of general war. Tensions were diffused when several Latin American nations sponsored a mediation conference. Huerta rejected its terms but soon lost power to Carranza, whom the United States accepted as the de facto head of government. The American occupation of Veracruz, which had brought Wilson savage criticism at home and abroad, ended the next month.

Relations between the United States and Mexico did not remain stable. As soon as Carranza ensconced himself in the presidential palace in Mexico City, several bandit chieftains with sizable armed forces rose to challenge his authority, notably Pancho Villa in Chihuahua Province to the north. By early 1916, incidents along the U.S.-Mexico border again tempted Wilson to consider an armed incursion into Mexico. Supporting intervention were influential American businesses holding Mexican properties and citizens in the American Southwest who worried about illegal immigrants and border raids.

For some time Villa's warrior-bandit force had harassed, robbed, and killed Americans on both sides of the Rio Grande. In early January 1916, it killed a group of American engineers working in Mexico. In March, Villa led a 500-man raid on Columbus, New Mexico, and struck a small American cavalry garrison, killing seventeen American soldiers and civilians. Shrill public and congressional calls for military action were followed by Wilson's dispatch of 158,000 troops to guard the border. With the reluctant approval of the Mexican president, Wilson also authorized a "punitive expedition" of 15,000 U.S. Army and National Guard soldiers, led by Brigadier General John J. ("Black Jack") Pershing, to pursue Villa in northern Mexico.

In luring Villa into a decisive battle, the operation was unsuccessful; unfortunately, the largest engagement took place between the American expedition and the Mexican Army instead of Villa's forces. As the Americans moved deeper into Mexico, Carranza became uncooperative and the Mexican people very hostile toward Pershing's troops and the Wilson administration. With a new Mexican constitution adopted and American entry into the World War looming, Wilson ordered the Mexican expedition withdrawn in early February 1917, leaving Villa at large.

Though an apparent failure, the operation did help to prepare the military and naval establishments for the war in France because it had identified problems in mobilization, training, and deployment. The performances of the commanders aided the administration in choosing leaders for the European war, with Pershing emerging as the leading candidate for the top command spot. The Mexican expedition also gave the military the opportunity to test weapons and equipment, including the relatively new military aircraft and recent models of motorized ground transportation. Even more so than the Veracruz experience, the anti-Villa operation showed the War and Navy departments the measure of their forces' combat readiness during the prelude to America's first large-scale overseas war.

With war raging in Europe and the United States intervening in various countries during the period 1914–1916, many American citizens became caught up in the excitement of a lively preparedness campaign. Although most Americans opposed intervention in Europe, public figures, special-interest organizations, and some influential newspapers backed a crusade to boost national defense. Among the leaders were former President Roosevelt, who also desired a troop command if war came, and Major General Leonard Wood, a former Army chief of staff with presidential ambitions. Many preparedness societies boasted members prominent in big business and politics.

After the sinking of the *Lusitania* in 1915, the preparedness campaign went into high gear. Wood persuaded the War Department to sponsor summer military training camps for civilians, beginning at Plattsburg, New York, that August. In arguing for preparedness, Wood compared the situation of the United States to a college athletic team that had "one good football player weighing about 110 pounds and another substitute perhaps turning the scales at 120 pounds. . . . They know they have got a game ahead with a first-class team trained to the hour and with at least five men for every position."

One of the most visible and strident crusaders for preparedness was Roosevelt, who summarized his views in his book *Fear God and Take Your Own Part.* He frequently targeted Wilson for his "weasel words" and his slowness to support the movement. The former president stated that he would stand by Wilson "so long as the President stands by the country." Roosevelt eventually moved from support of national defense to an open call for war because of violations to American neutrality. During the presidential election campaign of 1916, he spoke eloquently of "the shadows of the tortured dead" and "the shadows of the helpless whom Mr. Wilson did not dare to protect."

President Wilson initially resisted the agitation for preparedness, but by late 1915 he had begun to tour the country championing the concept of peacetime preparedness. He supported the efforts of other advocates who pressured Congress to enact legislation to fund large military and naval buildups. Throughout 1916 the preparedness supporters enjoyed victories on Capitol Hill. The National Defense Act, signed into law in June 1916, doubled the size of the Army to 223,000 officers and men and enlarged the National Guard, putting it under the War Department. It also funded Plattsburg-type summer training camps, set up the Reserve Officer Training Corps on college campuses, and provided for economic mobilization planning. Congress also authorized a program to construct a naval fleet "second to none"—an expectation that would not be realized in time for use in the Great War.

The Council of National Defense, an advisory body to the secretary of war, was established to oversee preparedness; it met for the first time in September 1916. The Shipping Act, signed by Wilson that same month, boosted federal aid to the lagging American merchant marine. Funding of the greatly enlarged military and naval programs was provided in part by the 1916 Revenue Act, which taxed especially well-to-do individuals and large corporations.

Opposing the preparedness movement were many progressives, who deplored Wilson's change of heart in supporting it. They equated preparedness with "the admitted evils of militarism," which they blamed for the current war and feared would push the United States into the conflict. Bryan denounced the increase in military spending on the grounds that "this nation does not need burglars' tools unless it intends to make burglary its business." Others believed that the focus on defense would hurt the reform movement at home, because the "slavery" to arms production would check "the growth of liberty, of democracy, of the coming of the kingdom of heaven on earth." The antagonism of progressives was further reinforced as their traditional enemies— the military establishment, large industrialists, and big bankers— strongly supported the preparedness movement.

Further resistance to the preparedness campaign came from major agricultural and labor organizations. Peace groups, such as the League to Limit Armament and the Woman's Peace Party, headed by Jane Addams, persisted in their antipreparedness advocacy. Addams asserted that "the sacrifice of life in warfare is unnecessary and wasteful." The sentiment in Europe, based on her observations, was that "this war was an old man's war; that the young men who were dying . . . were not the men who believed in the war." In late 1915, industrialist Henry Ford financed the sending of a "peace ship" to Europe in a highly publicized but vain (even vainglorious) effort to interest European leaders in negotiating a peace settlement. In spite of significant opposition, the principal funds, the most followers, and the key influences in Congress all belonged to the preparedness movement.

In the presidential contest of 1916, Wilson campaigned for reelection on a platform of prosperity, preparedness, and "peace with honor." His Democratic party, however, preferred the slogan "He kept us out of war," which many voters found more appealing. Many progressives who had not supported Wilson in 1912 now shifted their votes to him on the strength of his image as the "peace" candidate. The Republican party was deeply divided on the issues of progressivism and U.S. participation in the war, although its nominee, Charles Evans Hughes, held many views similar to Wilson's and ran on a party platform that called for U.S. neutrality as well as preparedness. Theodore Roosevelt, whose third-party candidacy on a progressive ticket in 1912 had helped Wilson win with a minority of the popular vote, returned to the

Republican party and was a factor in the 1916 campaign as well. His severe criticism of the president and his advocacy of U.S. intervention in Europe were used by Democrats to portray the Republicans as warmongers. A large group of Republicans, including many members of the sizable German-American community in the Midwest, strongly opposed any aid to the Allies. Even with the Republican party internally divided, the election was considered extremely close.

Wilson won reelection by a narrow margin in what appeared to be a cautious endorsement of his leadership at home and in foreign affairs. Most voters obviously favored preparedness, but by no means did they want to intervene in the World War. While the British marching song "Tipperary" was extremely popular, Americans also sang "I Didn't Raise My Boy to be a Soldier." Yet within four months of Wilson's reelection, the United States became embroiled in its first great global conflict.

America Enters the War

By the winter of 1916–1917, the mounting losses of fighting men compelled both the Central powers and the Allies to question how much longer the relentless war of attrition could continue. For all belligerents, morale became a disturbing factor at the front and at home, and mutiny in the armed forces caused rising anxiety. Criticism of the political and military leadership of the war mounted in all the nations at arms, though less publicly in the more militaristic states like Germany. By far, Germany had suffered the greatest human sacrifice among the Central powers. Its leaders knew that German military and naval strength had peaked and would continue to decline as its reservoir of young men headed toward depletion. No decision-makers in Europe were more vulnerable to taking a high-risk gamble than those in Berlin.

In the top echelons of Germany's government, the generals increasingly determined policy and strategy, further constricting the role of civilian officials such as Chancellor Bethmann Hollweg. Field Marshal Paul von Hindenburg, General Erich F. W.

Ludendorff, and the section chiefs of the German General Staff constituted the nucleus of the dominant military hierarchy. In Hindenburg's view, Bethmann Hollweg possessed a "flabbiness" of conviction about prosecuting the war and even favored a "soft peace," that is, compromises on postwar aggrandizements to obtain an end to hostilities.

From the perspective of the Central powers, the United States by late 1916 had clearly become a belligerent on the side of the Allies. The Central powers considered the increasing American logistical support of the Allies to be equally as damaging as any potential use of American armed forces in Europe. Efforts to augment U-boat construction had been underway in Germany for some time, although submarine attacks on noncombatant ships had been restricted since the previous spring. To European capitals, Wilson's reelection in November signaled the prospects of further American assistance to the Allies and risks of full American belligerency.

German leaders advanced plans for a large underseas offensive in the Atlantic in 1917, confident that their enlarged submarine fleet could interdict shipping between the United States and the Allies. In the German view, the loss of American supplies would so cripple the Allies that they would be forced to negotiate an end to the war. If American forces should be committed to the war before the Allies capitulated, German commanders believed the U-boats could prevent the shipment of troops to Europe.

One savage critic of the German supreme command's conduct of the war, Hans Delbrück, a brilliant civilian strategist, argued that the generals were ignoring the fundamental principle that politics and war are inextricably linked. As he put it, "No strategical idea can be considered completely without considering the political goal." The overconfident senior military officers dismissed the warnings of Delbrück, the Chancellor, and other civilians who opposed the acceleration of the war.

On January 9, 1917, the German high command, backed by Kaiser Wilhelm II, made the fateful decision to resume unrestricted U-boat warfare at the end of the month. The choice of what amounted to an undeclared naval war against the United

States, the principal neutral power, put Germany in the unmistakable role of aggressor in that relationship. By forcing America, in essence, to enter the fray, Germany also irretrievably upset the balance of manpower and firepower on the Western Front and ensured the eventual military collapse of the Central powers.

In the meantime, unaware of the continuing German determination to decide matters by force of arms, the American president had undertaken new peace initiatives soon after his reelection. In mid-December, Wilson requested all the major belligerents to list their war aims. Berlin responded with evasiveness, while London and Paris put forward such extreme demands that the Central powers were bound to reject them. Nonetheless, Wilson continued looking for ways to mediate, or for any other nonmilitary options. On January 22, 1917, he addressed the Senate with a message directed also to the belligerents, in which he pledged to strive for "peace without victory" and to seek compromises between the two embattled coalitions. He proclaimed that "only a peace between equals can last, a peace the very principle of which is equality, and a common participation in a common benefit." He also maintained that war could be made less likely in the future if the peace-loving nations turned to "collective security" in order to "make it impossible that any such catastrophe should ever overwhelm us again."

The German government notified the United States on January 31 that it would resume unrestricted submarine warfare the next day. The president broke diplomatic relations with Germany on February 3, and U-boats began to sink American merchant vessels, causing considerable loss of life. Later that month Wilson received another major shock when he learned about the "Zimmermann telegram," a German communication intercepted and decoded by British intelligence. In this message, German Foreign Minister Arthur Zimmermann instructed his ambassador in Mexico to explore an alliance with the Mexican government. If Germany and the United States went to war, the proposal went, Mexico was to declare war on America and also ask Japan to join the alliance. In return, Germany would give Mexico substantial financial aid and the American states of Texas, New Mexico, and Arizona. Furious, Wilson released the German missive to the press, and the country reacted with outrage. On March 20, Wilson's cabinet voted unanimously in favor of going to war, but the president still searched earnestly for another solution.

Wilson finally decided on the course of "righteous war." On the rainy evening of April 2, 1917, the weather appropriate to his mood, the president traveled to Capitol Hill. Contributing to the tense atmosphere, cavalry troops escorted the president while sentries manned machine guns along his route. Wilson asked Congress to declare war on Germany, emphasizing the intolerable nature of the German U-boat campaign which "has swept every restriction aside" and shown a "reckless lack of compassion or principle." Castigating the leadership in Berlin but not blaming the German people, he declared, "The present German submarine warfare against commerce is a warfare against mankind." He went on to disclaim any territorial aims and to stress that "the world must be made safe for democracy." Wilson spoke with the loftiest of intentions and the saddest of feelings about the course on which he was setting his nation.

Congress greeted Wilson's war message with tumultuous applause. Afterward he remarked to his secretary, "My message today was a message of death for our young men. How strange it seems to applaud that." On the very day of the president's address, a newspaper poll among members of the House of Representatives showed their sentiment, like that of the voters, overwhelmingly favored entering the war; but the representatives, like the public, opposed sending American soldiers into combat in Europe by a two-to-one margin.

Congressional support for war was not universal. Senator George W. Norris, a progressive, charged that financial interests were pushing the United States into war "to preserve the commercial right of American citizens to deliver munitions of war to belligerent nations." As a result, he said, "millions of our brethren must shed their lifeblood, millions of brokenhearted women must weep," and "millions of babes must die from hunger." Progressive Senator Robert M. La Follette protested that poor Americans would be "called upon to rot in the trenches" and recommended that the sons of those who promoted American involvement—

newspaper editors, bankers, and "manufacturers of ammunition and war supplies"—should serve first in the war. The first woman elected to Congress, Jeannette Rankin, also opposed American involvement; years later, she again cast a vote against U.S. entry into a world war.

Congress passed the war resolution overwhelmingly in both houses, with six senators and fifty congressmen voting in opposition. War against Germany began officially on April 6. At Wilson's insistence, the United States was designated an "Associated Power" rather than a full member of the Allied coalition.

In giving Congress his reasons for war, the president omitted several considerations that have fueled debate ever since. Among these were the economic and financial links with the Allies, the security threat to the nation, the impact of Allied propaganda, the pro-British bias of Wilson himself and the majority of Americans, and the ideological aspect of democracy battling autocracy. The fact remains, however, that Wilson would not have led the United States into the war if Germany had not launched its new submarine tactics, and, in turn, Germany would not have resorted to such a gamble if it had not been suffering so badly from losses sustained on the killing fields of the Great War. The desperation of its leaders and peoples led to the German decision for a collision course with the United States—a turning point in modern world affairs.

CHAPTER TWO

Over There

When the United States became embroiled in the World War in April 1917, neither the Allies nor the Central powers had good prospects. That month German U-boats sank 880,000 tons of Allied shipping. The convoy system, in which merchant vessels traveled in close formation flanked by warships, gradually reduced future losses, but until early 1918, the tonnage of Allied vessels sunk still exceeded that of new ships built.

On the ground the Allies fared no better. The Central powers hurled back two French offensives in the spring of 1917 with heavy losses, followed by mutinies in several French divisions. British drives in Flanders during the last half of the year, likewise, were stopped with terrible casualties. On the Eastern Front, the tsarist government of Nicholas II fell in March 1917, and Russian offensives were defeated that summer and fall. In November the Bolsheviks seized power in Russia and agreed the next month to an armistice with Germany, ending Russia's military role in the war. Meanwhile, much of northeast Italy fell to the Austrians after a mutually bloody victory at Caporetto in the autumn of 1917.

The Central powers also suffered in significant ways. Each month the Allied naval blockade became more effective. Already pinched by Allied naval superiority and battle depletion of its men and materiel, Germany was forced to shoulder a growing share of its coalition's war effort as Austria-Hungary, Turkey, and Bulgaria neared the end of their resources and will to fight. Although alarmingly short of reserves, too, Germany managed to keep an edge in troop strength on the Western Front, but the advantage was not adequate to produce a decisive breakthrough.

In Come the Yanks

For the first year the United States was at war, its principal military contribution was made by the Navy. The dominant American naval figure on the war scene was Vice Admiral William S. Sims, commander of American naval forces in Europe, who aggressively tried to get the Navy Department to increase his decision-making power, to provide him more men and ships, and to accept his ideas on improving antisubmarine, mining, and convoying tactics and logistical systems. Strikingly good-looking and a favorite of the media, Sims attracted widespread attention when he made dynamic calls for expansion and modernization of the U.S. Navy, not unlike William Mitchell's campaign for the Army Air Service. Long known in the Navy as an outspoken reformer, Sims generated a "battle of cables" with his superiors in Washington, Secretary of the Navy Josephus Daniels and Admiral William S. Benson, chief of naval operations. Criticizing their procrastination in readying the Navy for combat and in heeding his many demands, Sims appeared to be competing with Pershing, head of U.S. ground forces in France, in a contest to annoy their respective service chiefs. In the summer of 1918 Sims told a colleague that he found it "curious" that "the Navy Department should have watched a war for three years and been in a war for one and a half years without having organized a practical piece of machinery to carry on its work."

In contrast to his relationship with his American superiors, Sims worked so well with his British naval colleagues that he had to defend himself against the president's charge that he was too "pro-British" and was "owned by the Admiralty." In spite of this criticism, Sims and top British Admirals John R. Jellicoe and David Beatty continued to coordinate Anglo-American operations in the Atlantic Ocean and the North Sea. Most important, they developed the aforementioned convoy system, whereby American and British destroyers and other sub-chasers escorted merchantmen and troopships to protect them from enemy attacks. American battleships joined the Royal Navy's efforts against German surface raiders off the Irish coast and in the North Sea. American and British ships also safely delivered over 2 million American soldiers to Europe.

Another significant American naval contribution, again carried out in cooperation with the Royal Navy, was the laying of a 70,000-mine barrier across the North Sea to discourage the German Navy from trying to break out into the Atlantic shipping lanes. American naval aircraft also played a part in the war, conducting raids from English airfields against German U-boat bases on Belgium's coast. There was no major surface engagement involving the American Navy. Ironically, the U.S. naval establishment's largest combat role was on the land: The Marine Corps' 4th Brigade was assigned to the Army's forces in France, with Major General John A. Lejeune becoming the first Marine to command an Army division.

The cessation of hostilities was marred for the Navy by two unfortunate episodes. Some of Sims's vessels helped to escort the surrendered German Navy to the British naval base at Scapa Flow in the Orkney Islands, off northern Scotland, and to guard it there. In June 1919, the German sailors blew up their own ships at Scapa Flow, causing considerable casualties on both sides and preventing the ships' transfer to the Allies. The Navy's record was also tarnished in the war's aftermath by a bitter feud between Sims and Daniels. The admiral accused the Navy Department of "gross mismanagement" during the war, a charge subsequently supported by a congressional investigation. The still irate Sims refused all medals and honors earned during the conflict, as did several other senior officers.

Actually, the congressional committee's finding may not have done justice to Daniels' leadership. A progressive newspaper publisher in North Carolina, Daniels had no knowledge of the Navy when Wilson appointed him to head that department as a reward for his campaign work. He held the post for eight years, working hard and learning quickly. He demonstrated skill in management and overseeing his admirals with the notable exception of Sims and his supporters.

The War Department underwent a far stormier wartime experience. Its secretary, Newton D. Baker, not only was ignorant of the Army when selected in 1916, but remained so during his five-year tenure. Of the three Army chiefs of staff who served under him, the only strong and able one was General Peyton C. March, appointed in May 1918 just as the American Army was going into large-scale action in France. March had previously served in France as Pershing's artillery chief. He was combative and vain but very dedicated and ruthlessly efficient; he performed well under difficult circumstances and managed to hold his office until he was succeeded by Pershing in 1921. Baker did a poor job in mediating the many sharp personal and professional clashes that arose between March and Pershing. Their jobs as chief of staff and expedition commander conflicted and overlapped, having never been clearly defined; and Pershing held rank seniority over the military head of the Army. March refused to yield any of his authority to Pershing, reminding him that the forces he commanded in Europe were "only a part of the American army."

Baker also faced pioneering responsibilities in administering the nation's first extensive military-industrial complex. During the formative period American production and delivery were nearly paralyzed, forcing the American forces in France to acquire most of their artillery, tanks, and aircraft from the British and French. Actually, even a man better qualified than Baker might not have performed well, given the unprecedented nature of the secretary's monumental duties.

Like Daniels, Baker won his position because of his closeness to the president rather than his knowledge of the War Department. Wilson had liked him as a student and admired him as a progressive mayor of Cleveland. Surely Wilson could have found service secretaries far better qualified than Daniels or certainly Baker, but, instead, he demonstrated little interest in the workings of the military and naval establishments. The role of commander in chief, says a respected Wilson scholar, "was utterly foreign to his being."

Wilson, who had said in 1915 that he would oppose conscription in case of war, had changed his mind by February 1917 when diplomatic relations with Germany ruptured over the unrestricted U-boat warfare. Secretly he instructed Baker to have a draft bill ready if he should have to ask for a declaration of war. When in April the White House presented its proposal for conscription to Congress, some members of the president's own Democratic party, especially those from the isolationist western farm states, opposed it vociferously. States-rights interests in the South and the American Federation of Labor also fought the bill. The advantages that many saw in conscription were expressed by the *Washington Post,* which called it "in harmony" with democracy, because it "destroys distinctions between rich and poor. It insures efficiency in war, both at the front and at home. . . . It forces cowards to do their share." Both the House majority leader and the chairman of the House Military Affairs Committee opposed the draft, so Wilson had to rely on a leading House Republican to maneuver the bill to the floor. The measure finally won approval in both houses and was signed by Wilson in May 1917.

While Congress was still debating the draft measure, the War Department began plans to print and distribute registration blanks. It persuaded the public printer to print secretly 10 million registration blanks, which soon overflowed the Government Printing Office's storage space and filled the cellar of the Washington Post Office. Finally, the forms were mailed quietly to the thousands of sheriffs and mayors across the nation, with instructions for secrecy until the bill became law. Amazingly, knowledge of this high-handed action was kept confidential; the news would have been a godsend for congressmen opposing the draft.

In contrast to the injustices of the Civil War draft measure of 1863, the Selective Service Act of May 1917 eliminated such inequities as substitutes, purchased exemptions, and bounties, and assured that conscripts would serve for the duration of the war. To spare the Army any opprobrium connected with administering the draft, civilian draft boards composed of volunteers assumed this responsibility. Although these local boards could grant exemptions based mainly on essential occupations and family obligations, all males between the ages of 21 and 30 had to register. These ages were later extended from 18 to 45.

Baker told Wilson that he planned to use "a vast number of agencies throughout the country to make the day of registration [June 5, 1917] a festival and a patriotic occasion." He secured the enthusiastic assistance of state and municipal organizations, local chambers of commerce, and the federal government's Committee on Public Information in promoting registration. The result was the registration of over 10 million young men, of whom the Army eventually drafted 2.7 million.

At first there was widespread volunteering of men who expected early draft calls because of the numbers issued to them in conscription drawings in July 1917. Local draft boards complained vehemently about the confusion in their plans caused by such actions. So the War Department announced in December that it would accept no more volunteers and would rely henceforth solely on the draft to fill the Army. By the end of the war, nearly 70 percent of the soldiers were draftees. In August 1918 Congress authorized the Navy and Marines to resort to conscription, though they actually drafted few men.

An important addition to the draft procedure was the "work or fight" order of May 1918, an amendment to the Selective Service regulations. It empowered draft boards to conscript every able-bodied man not effectively employed, regardless of classification or drawing number. It was issued because of public indignation at idlers who had been lucky in having their numbers come up near the last of the official drawings. The government drew up a list of "nonproductive occupations," which included such jobs as ushers, waiters, building attendants, and sales clerks.

Often community pressure in the form of alert, patriotic neighbors helped to enforce draft regulations. One draft board received so many complaints about the occupational exemption granted a beekeeper that it reversed its decision and sent him to the Army. Another board disallowed dependency claims upon learning that the allegedly dependent wives were taking in money from prostitution.

Among the requests for draft exemptions was that of a man who claimed that his manufacture of gopher traps was "essential to the welfare of the nation." A college student stated as his reason for exemption, "Ain't finished my studies." An item on the form for those requesting an occupational exemption read, "State why you can not be easily replaced by another person." One man wrote in response, "Nobody wants to take care of another man's wife."

Draft boards usually had strong community backing and used their powers to enforce local criteria of justice. For instance, the chairman of a board wrote, "One of the most pleasant duties of this board was to make good-for-nothing husbands support their wives." Often the boards found that women who opposed their husbands' being drafted yielded later when they learned they could get $30 or more a month while their men were in the Army. On the other hand, the wife of one farmer told his draft board: "My George ain't for sale or rent to no one. If he goes, I got to go too. I don't want your money—I jist wants George." When George failed his physical examination, she stuck out her tongue at the board chairman.

The Selective Service Act exempted as conscientious objectors only those men who were members of a "well recognized religious sect . . . whose existing creed or principles forbid its members to participate in war in any form." Baker later interpreted this to include men who had "personal scruples against war." Yet, in all cases, objectors were expected to accept alternative national service as stipulated by the War Department. Conscientious objectors numbered only 3,900, most of whom accepted the option of noncombatant service, furloughs to work on farms, or assignment to the Society of Friends Reconstruction Unit in France. About 500 objectors received prison terms; most of these were released not long after the armistice.

There seemed to be two main attitudes toward conscientious objectors. Theodore Roosevelt expressed what was probably the majority's viewpoint: "The bulk are slackers, pure and simple, or else traitorous pro-Germans." Baker, representing the other attitude, reported to Wilson that he had just talked to a number of objectors at Camp Meade, Maryland, adding, "Only two of those with whom I talked seemed quite normal mentally." In the course of the war many who first registered as conscientious objectors later changed their minds; and some of these men saw combat, including the most-decorated American soldier of the war, Alvin C. York.

The Selective Service Act established the broad outlines of the Army's structure for the war's duration. Its three parts were to be the Regular Army, the National Guard, and the new National Army of wartime volunteers and draftees. Much of the identity of these three groups eventually was lost as recruits and draftees alike were absorbed in all units, and in mid-1918 the War Department changed the designation of all land forces to one "United States Army." By the end of the war, the Army included more than 3.5 million men.

American troops sent to Europe were organized as the American Expeditionary Forces (AEF), which eventually numbered more than 2 million men. Appointed to head the AEF was Pershing, who as the leader of the recent Mexican expedition had emerged as the War Department's logical choice to command the AEF. Tough, experienced, ambitious, and highly professional, he reported to the War Department in early May 1917. Baker, who had not met him before, approved of him because he appeared healthy and vigorous.

Pershing arrived in Paris in mid-June with fewer than 200 officers and men, the nucleus of his headquarters. Field Marshal Haig later wrote that "1917 was a most critical period, and the arrival of General P. and a few officers of his staff in that summer produced a most heartening effect on both ourselves and the French." Crowds in Paris mobbed Pershing's motorcade, throwing flowers, waving handkerchiefs, and shouting "Vive l'Amérique." During his first weeks in France, Pershing, a dignified figure with erect military bearing, further captured the imagination of the French people when he visited Napoleon's tomb and ceremoniously kissed the emperor's sword.

After an American battalion paraded through Paris in a Fourth of July celebration, Pershing laid a wreath on the grave of the Marquis de Lafayette, the French general who had helped the United

States win independence from the British. One of Pershing's aides told the spectators, "Lafayette, we are here," a phrase which came to symbolize the American commitment to Europe. Unforeseen by the enthusiastic crowds, another year would elapse before American forces would enter combat in large numbers.

Pershing set up his headquarters in Chaumont, southeast of Paris, and began to organize the future American army. He insisted on a separate sector for the AEF because he intended, in accordance with his orders from Washington, to keep the Americans as a distinct fighting force. His continuing determination to do this appalled the British and French leaders, who had suffered heavy manpower losses for many years and had hoped to use the fresh American troops to bolster existing Allied divisions along the Western Front. Allied commanders did not believe the AEF would be ready to handle a separate area of the front for a long time, if ever, and they viewed the creation of an American army as a waste of time they could not afford to lose. Pershing steadfastly resisted Allied efforts to commit his forces in such piecemeal fashion and argued stubbornly that a distinct American front be established when his divisions were combat-ready. In his insistence Pershing was perhaps more lucky than wise at times, for if the tide of war had shifted slightly in favor of the Germans, his AEF could have faced deep trouble before attaining coordination with flanking Allied forces.

By the fall of 1917 most American forces were stationed in the provinces of Alsace and Lorraine, a quiet area where the soldiers could receive the additional training that Pershing now realized was needed. He reluctantly agreed to use Allied instructors who favored trench warfare, but he ordered them to emphasize attack, not defense, tactics. American criticism of European warfare was summed up by Major General Robert L. Bullard, who told Pershing: "Trench warfare, if prolonged beyond a very limited period, takes the offensive spirit out of troops." Under British and French advisers, the training program intensified. Pershing's revised schedule called for the 1st Infantry Division to enter the frontline trenches in December and the other three divisions six months later.

In his position as commander of the AEF, Pershing proved to be hard-driving and strict in dealing with his men, who respected him as a dedicated and forceful professional soldier. To Allied high commanders, however, as well as to some of his own senior officers, he sometimes appeared aloof, austere, impatient, and even ruthless. On a number of occasions he found himself in trouble simultaneously with March and his staff in Washington and with top British and French leaders on the Western Front, though for different reasons. When Pershing clashed with the Allies on such issues as amalgamation of forces and the importance of offensive operations, his dogged stubbornness and short temper were decided liabilities. In his diary Haig described Pershing as "very obstinate and stupid."

As Pershing built his AEF organization, he faced other pressures. Former President Roosevelt demanded a division command, based on his quite limited combat experience with the fabled "Rough Riders," a cavalry regiment in the Spanish-American War. His health was poor—he would die in early 1919—so the Wilson administration was able to reject him without creating too big a furor. With an eye on the next presidential race, General Wood, the former chief of staff, sought an AEF command slot. Surprisingly, he passed his physical; somehow Pershing managed to avoid giving an appointment to this distinguished but fiery commander far past his military prime. As the fighting grew fiercer and the stress on Pershing greater, the War Department sent a number of generals on month-long "tours" of the battlefront (usually rear areas only) for Pershing to "inspect" for possible AEF appointments. At this time he also had the distracting duty of hosting legions of American and Allied politicians and other public figures who visited France. Fortunately, he could meet many of them in Paris rather than at his Chaumont headquarters.

In the meantime, Pershing carefully selected his top lieutenants. He relied heavily on Brigadier General James G. Harbord, an excellent chief of staff and his closest advisor, to organize the huge staff structure and training programs of the AEF for future large-scale warfare. Later the invaluable Harbord headed the AEF logistical arm, the Services of Supply. Pershing chose strong advocates of the two "weapons of the future" to play principal roles: Colonel George S. Patton, Jr., directed the AEF Tank Corps' training center, while Brigadier General William Mitchell commanded the AEF Air Service and later the air combat forces.

Patton, one of the first AEF officers to reach France, was an aggressive, colorful figure who soon impressed a British commander as "a fireater [who] longs for the fray." Patton's ambition led him to seek the tank assignment as a way to enter combat and to advance his career. Although he later became firmly convinced of the tank's value in war, at first he doubted the new technology, writing his father: "There is about a fifty percent chance they wont work at all but if they do they will work like hell. . . . In the tanks you are not apt to be wounded. You either get blown to bitts by a direct hit or you are not touched." The AEF used French and British tanks in combat, with the first American-made tank arriving in France a few days after the armistice.

The AEF air arm began arriving in France in September 1917 and immediately confronted a staggering number of problems: airfields had to be constructed; aircraft, spare parts, and trained personnel were inadequate in numbers and quality; and, perhaps most important, the AEF placed the priority on building up ground forces rather than air forces to combat readiness. Mitchell, described by colleagues as a "bundle of energy," worked tirelessly for the air forces in France, but not until spring 1918 did American patrols inaugurate regular observation and intercept missions in the relatively quiet sectors assigned to the AEF. Facing the same situation as the Tank Corps, they flew British and French planes.

In June 1918, American forces had enough aircraft to contribute significantly to the aerial support at Chateau Thierry and Belleau Wood, just northeast of Paris. By the time American forces undertook major offensives in the fall, AEF aircraft participated in ground-support and behind-the-lines bombing, strafing, and artillery spotting. When the hostilities ended, most of the AEF's 5,200 aircraft (almost all French) were obsolete, and many were burned as scrap in France in what was nicknamed the "Billion Dollar Bonfire."

Although after the war Mitchell became famous as a crusader for American military aviation and its strategic potential, the most celebrated AEF combat airman was Edward V. Rickenbacker, a fighter pilot with the 94th "Hat in the Ring" Squadron. The out-fit became renowned for its daring exploits, especially against "Red Baron" Manfred von Richthofen's "Flying Circus" Squadron, whose planes were distinguished by red noses, white tails, and red stripes (the last indicating the number of planes downed). Rick-enbacker, a professional race car driver before the war, began his AEF career as Pershing's chauffeur. By May 1918, he headed the squadron and had become an "ace" (downing five enemy planes). His most impressive achievement occurred that September when he took on seven German aircraft and destroyed two of them, a feat that earned him the Medal of Honor.

Pershing's grand plan for preparing his forces to enter combat as a fully trained, separate American army was interrupted by German actions in the spring and summer of 1918. Having formally ended its war with Russia on the Eastern Front by the Treaty of Brest-Litovsk on March 3, 1918, Germany had superior man-power and firepower on the Western Front. Field Marshal von Hindenburg and General Ludendorff decided to launch a series of ambitious "end the war" offensives to attain victory on the West-ern Front before the AEF could get fully into action and thus offset the German advantages. They recognized the dangers of the in-creasingly effective Allied naval blockade, the weakening of the German submarine campaign, and the mounting arrivals of Ameri-can troops in France.

The first of the five German "end-the-war" offensives in 1918 began on March 21 along a sixty-mile front in the Somme Valley, its aim to split British and French forces and break through to the English Channel. The Somme offensive carried forty miles deep into the Allied lines before it was stopped with horrendous losses on both sides. As a consequence of the massive German threat, the Allied Supreme War Council named its first overall commander, French Marshal Ferdinand Foch.

Fortunately for Pershing and his AEF, Foch appraised them more generously than did many senior French and British leaders.

Already irate at Pershing for his resistance to amalgamating American troops with their forces in combat, the Allied commanders intensified their criticism when the German offensives began. They warned that the Germans might win the war before Pershing fully developed the AEF and committed it to action. In vain efforts repeated throughout the rest of the war, French Premier Georges Clemenceau, known as "the Tiger" for his fierceness in French political and military affairs, asked Wilson to remove Pershing for his uncooperative attitude, while the British, also to no avail, tried to have the AEF placed under their command.

Near the end of the Somme crisis, Pershing discreetly compromised and offered the new supreme commander his eight combat-ready divisions for service with Allied troops. Haig wrote bitterly: "I hope the Yankees will not disappoint us in this. They have seldom done anything yet which they have promised." He charged that Pershing "did not seem to realise the urgency of the situation." Foch, however, came to appreciate Pershing's stress on offensive training and on his goal of commanding a separate American sector.

The Lys offensive, Ludendorff's second major drive, struck British positions in the Lys Valley of Flanders but was repulsed, too, after severe fighting in April. The next month the German Aisne offensive penetrated deeply into the Aisne and Marne valleys and advanced to a point only fifty miles from Paris. The surprising German success led Ludendorff to commit more divisions to the drive, while the French Army hastily reinforced the region. The Allies, including American troops, finally halted the Germans in mid-June.

During the Aisne drive, the AEF participated strongly in combat for the first time. North of Paris, American soldiers captured the village of Cantigny and held it against a powerful counterattack. According to Colonel George C. Marshall, then serving in division headquarters: "The heights of Cantigny were of no strategic importance, and of small tactical value. This issue was a moral one. This was our first offensive." To him Cantigny "demonstrated conclusively the fighting qualities and fortitude of the American soldier." It also strengthened Pershing's case for a distinct American sector.

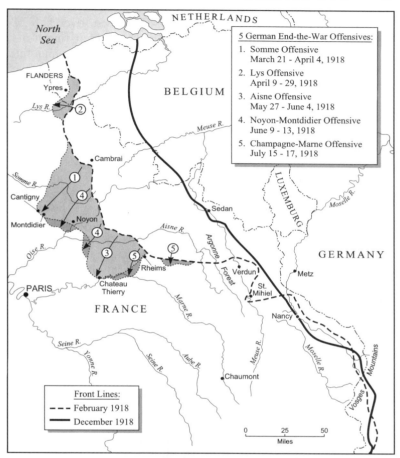

Western Front: German End-the-War Offensives, March–July 1918

Also during the Aisne action, the first sizable American battle occurred at Chateau Thierry and nearby Belleau Wood, when American Army and Marine forces helped the French stop the German push toward Paris. While suffering almost 10,000 casualties, the Americans took both the town and forest. As Marines crossed fields of poppies prior to an attack, one sergeant yelled, "Come on, you sons of bitches. Do you want to live forever?" The

Belleau Wood action cost the Marines 4,600 men, over half of their brigade. Meanwhile, the Germans launched their fourth offensive in the Noyon-Montdidier area to the northwest, which the French stopped with the assistance of Americans. By then, more than 300,000 American troops were arriving in France each month.

Although the German Army on the Western Front was badly shaken and its shock troops depleted, Ludendorff ordered the launching of the Champagne-Marne offensive, his fifth drive. It began on July 15, with German spearheads crossing the Marne River on both sides of the strategic city of Rheims. The main defenders were French, but about 85,000 American soldiers were involved. After five days of severe fighting the Germans' last drive was spent. The frantic "end-the-war" offensives had cost the Germans a half million of their troops. The Allies lost more men but had abundant reserves, now that the Americans were there in force. The turning point on the Western Front had now been reached, and Ludendorff dejectedly prepared to withdraw his forces from the large salient north of Paris and cancel his plans for yet another offensive.

Meanwhile Foch ordered a combined French and American force to counterattack in the Aisne-Marne region. Massive Allied assaults began on July 18, before Ludendorff could get his soldiers out of the salient. One American waiting for his unit to enter battle described the intensive artillery fire already underway: "Away over where the enemy's position was I seen a cloud of smoke and dust boiling up. All along that line was flickerings like heat lightening and it made a sort of bubbling sound, like oatmeal when it boils. That was the shells bursting. It was sure nice." Large American forces helped the French to cut off the German salient and eliminate it by August 6. As a new British drive opened two days later to the northwest, Ludendorff reported to Berlin that "the black day of the German Army" was at hand and "the war must be ended." His superiors decided, instead, to continue the fight.

By August 10, Pershing had enough trained troops to form the American First Army, which would fight as a distinct force on its own area of the front as he had long wished. In addition to this army, significant numbers of American troops served with British and French forces throughout the final stages of the war. About 1,000 Americans also were attached to the Italian Army, although Pershing recalled most of them for the last few months of the war.

With some personal trepidation and against the strong misgivings of other Allied commanders, Foch finally approved Pershing's plan for his new First Army, together with a French colonial corps, to reduce the St. Mihiel salient, below Verdun. Foch feared that it might delay the AEF's participation in the huge Allied offensive set for late September, but Pershing assured him that his army could capture its objective in time to join the larger offensive. The area targeted by Pershing had been held by the Germans since early in the war, in spite of many French efforts to retake it. Ludendorff, alerted by the nearby buildup of over a half million American and French soldiers, ordered the area evacuated, but five understrength German divisions were still there when the AEF offensive began.

In the largest American Army campaign since the Civil War, the First Army struck on September 12. Pershing's forces captured the St. Mihiel salient in five days against moderate resistance. Some jubilant AEF field commanders wanted to press on north to seize the strategic rail center of Metz, but Pershing refused, in keeping with his commitment to Foch. Instead, he began an extraordinary movement of his men sixty miles to the northwest for the Meuse-Argonne offensive, set to begin only two weeks after the securing of the St. Mihiel bulge.

Colonel George Marshall, the brilliant operational planning officer who served as Army chief of staff in World War II, handled the complex logistical problems of the AEF move from St. Mihiel to the Meuse-Argonne sector, winning praise from Pershing and the nickname "the Wizard." Marshall oversaw the deployment of 600,000 fresh American soldiers into the Meuse-Argonne line while the St. Mihiel operation was still underway. Then he managed the intricate shift of 220,000 French and other Allied troops from that sector and the transfer of another 600,000 AEF troops from St. Mihiel and southern areas to the Meuse-Argonne lines. In spite of heavy rains, many green soldiers, and few roads (and those in poor shape), Marshall accomplished the gargantuan task and got the men in their assigned positions on time. One of the most difficult feats was the movement of AEF units just to the rear of the frontlines, even while the St. Mihiel operation was still in progress; it was achieved by traveling at night without lights, hazardous on bad roads in rugged terrain even without combat nearby.

With more than 1 million Americans participating, the Meuse-Argonne campaign, September 26–November 11, 1918, was the largest and costliest in the American Army's annals up to then, as well as the single most decisive Allied operation of the war. To the west and northwest, British, French, and Belgian armies launched simultaneous assaults as the AEF's First Army, with the French Fourth Army on its left, began the thrust into the most foreboding enemy defenses on the entire Allied front. Invaluable to the quick German deployment of mobile reserves was a railroad that ran along much of the front in the enemy's rear; it came closest to the frontline in the AEF sector, where it was strongly guarded. That area was distinctive not only for its three heavily fortified defensive lines but also for the unusually dense woods, steep hills, and precipitous ravines that made the AEF's path the most difficult facing any of the Allied armies.

All the Allied forces in the lineup from the English Channel to the Meuse River moved out on schedule on September 26, with everyone except the Americans making considerable progress. In the AEF sector, the Germans resisted so savagely that the Americans had to resort to bloody frontal attacks, leaving many units battered and stalled. One soldier wrote that "the poor boys were getting slaughtered as fast as sheep could go up a plank." The Germans "made our company look like a squad; all that was left was a handful of men." German reinforcements added to the desperate situation, especially for the untried American troops. On October 3, Pershing temporarily halted the attacks in the Argonne Forest, though his troops had penetrated two of the German defensive lines and were approaching the last and strongest one.

Pershing later said that this time "involved the greatest strain on the army and on me." Allied leaders renewed their pressure on Pershing to yield command of his troops to them. Clemenceau

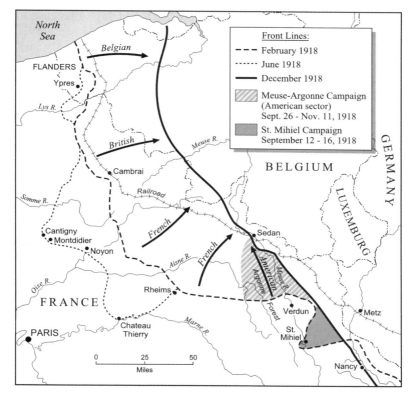

Western Front: Allied Offensives, September–November, 1918

wrote Foch that the American troops were not "unusable; they are merely unused," criticism that Foch rejected. Pershing relieved several divisional and regimental commanders, while veteran soldiers replaced many of the men who had just been through their first combat, suffering from exhaustion, injuries, the effects of cold weather, and influenza and pneumonia, which were devastating the troops.

On October 4, the First Army resumed its advance, still undergoing heavy bloodletting but gradually progressing in the tough terrain. The following week, Pershing assigned the new American

Second Army to undertake an offensive on the high ground east of the Meuse River. The drive overran German observation and artillery positions that had vexed the First Army to the west. By late October, the AEF had penetrated the final German line and was poised to close to the Meuse River. Across it lay Sedan, the historic city where the French Army had surrendered to the Germans in 1871.

The commander of the French Fourth Army, approaching Sedan on the west flank of the AEF divisions, expected to have the honor of capturing the city, a long-desired goal of Frenchmen. When the final phase of the Meuse-Argonne offensive got underway on November 1, however, the astonishingly light resistance by the Germans suddenly transformed the hard-fought campaign into a race by American and French divisions to seize Sedan, causing great confusion and even reckless conduct in action. AEF headquarters precipitated the situation by ordering divisions in the vanguard to disregard divisional boundaries in their pursuit of the enemy across the Meuse. On November 6, the race for Sedan turned into a near disaster. Suddenly the American 1st Division began an astonishing move across the fronts of the one French and two American divisions close to Sedan. Thinking the 1st Division was a German force, all three divisions opened fire; their target, the 1st, boasted a distinguished history and a membership that had included Pershing and many of his senior officers.

Adding to the confusion, soldiers of the 1st discovered a flamboyantly attired officer examining a map in a field below the Meuse. They thought he was "an old-style Prussian general" and captured him in spite of his protests. Back at division headquarters the prize prisoner was detained until it was proven that he was Brigadier General Douglas MacArthur, a much-decorated, if outraged, brigade commander of the 42nd Division who often dressed somewhat out of accord with regulations. The Sedan debacle brought no serious repercussions, such as a Chaumont investigation or court-martial of any officers involved, possibly because the senior officers were all close to Pershing, but more likely because the retreating Germans were not able to profit by the pandemonium. In the end, Sedan was not captured by any of the divisions in the race but was occupied quietly by the French after the armistice.

The Meuse-Argonne campaign, as well as the earlier American operations, produced many individual and group actions marked by extraordinary valor. None was more spectacular than the achievement of Private York from Pall Mall, Tennessee. On October 8, 1918, as the AEF forces fought their way through heavily defended German positions in the Argonne wilderness, York's patrol ran into intense fire, was surrounded, and suffered casualties of 50 percent of its men. York took temporary charge and somehow managed to extricate the patrol survivors from what seemed to be certain death or capture. In the process he personally knocked out thirty-five German machine guns, killing twenty of the enemy "the way we shoot wild turkeys at home." York returned to American lines with so many German prisoners that he had to march them "double-time" to reach a prisoner compound large enough to handle them. He recounted that the brigade commander told him, "'Well, York, I hear you have captured the whole damned German army.' And I told him I only had 132." Marshal Foch, the Allied supreme commander, praised York's feat as "the greatest accomplishment by any private soldier of all the armies of Europe" during the war. He received the Medal of Honor, numerous Allied decorations, and promotion to sergeant, besides acclamation in the United States as the nation's foremost hero of the Great War.

Fighting on the Western Front ceased at 11:00 A.M. on November 11, 1918, in accordance with an armistice signed several hours earlier. The AEF's participation had tipped the balance of troops and firepower in favor of the Allies at a critical time on the Western Front. American forces were essential to turning back the final German drives and in the success of the last, most decisive Allied offensive of the entire war. Additionally, the promise of American troops had strongly affected both the Allies and the Central powers. The United States Navy also played a significant role in making the convoy system work, laying the North Sea mine barrier, and thus assuring the security of the American lifeline to Britain and France.

Total American combat casualties in the Great War were 342,000, including ground, sea, and air personnel. Those killed in action numbered 49,000, but the total death toll was over 112,000, the rest dying mainly from diseases, especially during the devastating influenza-pneumonia epidemic of the fall of 1918. For the period the Americans were heavily engaged in combat, from May to November 1918, the AEF's casualties were proportionately higher than those sustained by any of the other armies. While the American cost in lives was serious, it was relatively small compared to those of the European belligerents: nearly 9 million civilians and 8 million troops. The far greater price paid by the Europeans is one of the main reasons European histories of World War I tend to discount the American contribution to victory.

Pershing, like several other Allied chiefs, thought the armistice was a strategic blunder and favored a march to Berlin to defeat the Germans decisively. He claimed that if "given another ten days we would have rounded up the entire German army, captured it, humiliated it." Until he left Europe in September 1919, he kept his occupation forces in the Rhineland on alert for news of a breakdown in the peace talks, whereupon he and the other Allied occupation commanders were to take over all of Germany.

Upon his return to the States, Pershing received the new rank of "General of the Armies" and later became the Army chief of staff. He served as the role model, policy and personnel adviser, and sponsor of many promising officers who would reach the zenith of their careers in the Second World War. In unbroken succession from 1918 to 1945, the American Army chiefs of staff were men who had served in the AEF. They, especially Pershing and Marshall, cast long shadows over the shaping of the modern American military establishment. They also influenced the American strategic priority on Western Europe as essential to the security of the United States.

Emergence of the Citizen-Soldier

The progressive spirit was quite apparent in the training of America's citizen-soldiers (draftees, war volunteers, reservists, and National Guardsmen) of 1917–1918. As Wilson remarked in April 1918, "I do not believe it an exaggeration to say that no army ever before assembled has had more conscientious and painstaking thought given to the protection and stimulation of its mental, moral, and physical manhood." The president's words set the evangelical tone of the crusade not only to spread democracy globally but also to mold American recruits according to progressive standards. He, Baker, and Raymond Fosdick, head of the Commission on Training Camp Activities, were determined that this great force of citizen-soldiers would be morally better than armies of the past; it would not, for example, be contaminated by the traditional vices of liquor and prostitutes. Both Baker and Fosdick were former urban officials known for their progressive zeal, and they enlisted local communities, camp newspapers, public health officials, church groups, and YMCA workers to set up "vice-free zones" around the fast-growing training cantonments. They interfered with individual liberties, but it was high-minded meddling. It would be ridiculous to suggest that the recruits were not exposed to worldly temptations, but the progressive leadership in the War Department maintained a persistent campaign against booze and women of the streets.

The draft act may have been written as fairly as possible at the time, but the resulting conscription, for a number of complex reasons, tended to take men from below average social and economic levels. About 30 percent of the draftees could not read or write. The majority's scores on Army intelligence tests were about equal to that of the average white seventh-grader. Allowing for the social bias of the tests, the experience and social sophistication of most of the enlisted men were very limited. Young, poorly educated, and often from farms, they were both confused and high-spirited, which made them pliable material for authorities to mold into an army to send to France and also a force to help bolster certain values in the postwar era.

The Army educated its troops in a number of ways. It introduced them to indoor plumbing, which 60 percent of the draftees had not experienced before their induction. It imposed hygiene standards on them in training camp, as described by a new soldier writing his mother: "The government requires us to bathe at least 3 times a week, to change underclothes every 2 days, and sox daily, and to keep clean-shaven." The Army informed its troops about venereal diseases and taught many of them trades, as well as instructing a sizable number of them how to read. Also, the Army taught immigrants to speak English; one out of six draftees had not been born in the United States. In addition, nearly half of the draftees had to be taught to play such team sports as baseball and football. The military demanded obedience but also sought to persuade the recruits that American institutions were superior to all others.

Basically, the Army and assisting civilian agencies imposed middle-class standards of living and values on draftees in the training camps. This introduced a considerable number of men to new ways of life and indeed provided many a gateway to the middle class. The jumble of new experiences and values, no doubt, awed and confused many of the native-born draftees who had left their home communities for the first time. As a train loaded with draftees en route to camp was traveling fifty miles west of Danville, Virginia, an amazed mountaineer who had been drafted and had boarded at Danville exclaimed to the man beside him, "Bud, if this old world is as big the other way as she is this, she's a hell-buster for sartain."

Adjustment to the military's way of doing things could be unnerving. One recruit was shocked the first day, writing home to his mother: "First we were physically examined, vaccinated, inoculated, borated, carbolated, blockaded, and mustered in." A former seminary student wrote his parents: "Good heavens! Two weeks ago I was studying Aristotle and Christian Ethics; this afternoon I have been learning to use a bayonet—just how to jab a man—to aim for his stomach first and always to twist the bayonet before pulling it out." All had to learn that the greatest tradition of the Army is "hurry up and wait," whether standing outside in a grub line during a downpour or waiting hours for a turn on the firing line after arriving there at double time.

The minute-man myth suggests that most American boys are marksmen, but in 1917–1918 many assigned to the infantry had never shot a rifle. A serious shortage of small arms and artillery weapons hampered training in the United States through much of the short time the country was in the war. The scarcity of rifles forced drilling with wooden sticks for a while, but even when the supply of rifles increased, the rush calls for divisions to go to embarkation ports prevented many recruits from firing their weapons prior to their arrival in France. In June 1918 an AEF inspector reported that 40 percent of the infantrymen of one division had not yet fired a rifle, even during training in France; in another division the total was 45 percent.

The combination of overcrowding in large cantonments and the relatively backward state of medicine brought affliction to many and death to some in the ranks. Measles, diarrhea, mumps, tuberculosis, chicken pox, smallpox, typhoid, meningitis, and diphtheria all hit epidemic levels in various camps despite efforts to enforce camp sanitation and preventive medicine. The worst, as mentioned, was the epidemic of flu and pneumonia that swept the United States and Europe in the fall of 1918. At its peak in early October, 4 out of every 1,000 soldiers in the United States died from what was popularly called "Spanish influenza," an especially virulent strain of the disease that severely struck active young adults. Hardest hit was Camp Sherman, Ohio, where 40 percent of the troops at the post had flu or pneumonia, and over 1,100 of them died in seventeen days. Chief of Staff March notified Pershing on November 5 that "influenza not only stopped all draft calls in October but practically stopped all training." Compared to the training camps in the United States, the AEF camps lost fewer men, but still 12,400 American troops in France died from flu or pneumonia during the epidemic. In all, the American military forces of the First World War lost more men to influenza and pneumonia than to death in combat.

Divisional training in France was much more rigorous than it had been in the States, for Pershing and his headquarters staff at Chaumont were hard task-masters, bent on proving to the skeptical, veteran French and British forces that the "doughboys"* could measure up. Usually the training schedule at AEF rear-area camps

---

*The origin of the term "doughboys" is enigmatic. According to one explanation, it originated among American troops patrolling the Rio Grande shortly after the Mexican Revolution erupted in 1911. American infantry marching through south Texas often complained about the choking white dust of the adobe soil that covered their uniforms. Cavalry troops derisively nicknamed them "adobes," which soon became "dobies" and finally "doughboys." Another explanation is that soldiers' buttons in the late 1860s resembled "doughboys." The term continued to be used for American infantrymen in France in 1917–1918 and eventually became a nickname for all AEF soldiers.

took up ten hours a day, six days a week, but there were also unbroken two-day stretches in practice trenches before departure for
quiet sectors of the front in Alsace and Lorraine. When the French
first demonstrated to one American regiment the use of flame-
throwers and poison-gas devices, an observer said that many of the
doughboys loudly denounced such weapons as "cowardly and in-
humane." Once in action, however, they generally dropped such
scruples. MacArthur's brigade, for example, took pride in the fact
that for every poison-gas projectile that the Germans fired at them,
they sent back at least two in return.

One AEF officer said of the soldiers training under him in
France: "Theirs was the spirit of a youngster out squirrel-shooting
with his first rifle. Left to their own initiative, they would have
kept a stream of shells in the air with all the prodigality of the
small boy who expends his firecrackers before breakfast on the 4th
of July in order to show 'old Henry Boche,' as they called him,
that they were on the job." Another observer said that the morale
of the Americans was "incredibly high" in the Lorraine camps:
"Many had the idea that the war would be over before they would
ever get into the trenches." They were intensely impatient to en-
gage the Germans, some fearing "that all this drilling would be as
futile as carrying water from a creek to the top of a hill and allowing it to flow back into the creek." A British veteran wryly commented that the Yanks' enthusiasm was based on the same illusion
that the new British recruits had nourished in August 1914.

The adjustment of the AEF troops to the French and British
was quite uneven, depending upon each individual's experience.
For some reason, the Americans who trained and fought alongside
the British Army developed deeper, more widespread dislike for
the "limeys" than did the much larger number of AEF troops associated with French units. One AEF veteran recalled, "Australians
and Canadians seemed to share this feeling and, on occasion, in
bar-room brawls in the French villages behind the lines, they
would join with the Yanks against the English." According to one
soldier, he and his buddies were rankled by the pretension of the
British and by their language: "What American soldier would
guess that when a British officer reported from the front—'Things

here are a bit fruity'—that he meant that his unit had suffered heavy casualties."

In contrast, the Americans and the French villagers, who were mostly old men and women with grandchildren swarming about them, got along famously. An unusually strong bond developed between the AEF soldiers and the French children. One American veteran observed:

The spell which the children of France exerted over every [American] soldier from the first was not alone due to the sympathy which their smiles . . . aroused on the background of war. We found that, whether the children came from chateaux or from alleys, they had as a birthright that indescribable thing most difficult of acquirement and most truly French—charm. . . . It was from [the] children that the soldiers largely learned their French, though not in the manner of a powerfully built corporal I have in mind, seated in a doorway, knitting his brows over his primer which made French easy in a few lessons. He drew up on his lap, much as a big dog would lift a puppy, a little girl who had been sitting at his feet regarding him as she would an inhabitant from another world.

"Say, kid, is this right?" he asked, as he read off an exercise according to his own [terrible] phonetic pronunciation.

"Oui! Oui!" said the child, who thought that he was still speaking English; and thus they continued the lesson happily together.

The French, in turn, picked up some dubious tidbits of miscellaneous information about the United States from the Americans. One old veteran estimated that in talking to attractive French peasant girls at least 90 percent of such fortunate doughboys claimed that they were from Mississippi—simply because they loved to hear the young women say "Meeseeseepee." The ways of the Americans sometimes baffled the French peasants. One AEF soldier, for instance, described the astounded look on an old Frenchman's face "in the chill frost of a Lorraine dawn" as he watched a company of troops "stream down from boxcars, strip to the waist, and sluice themselves at the horse trough. If this was not an indication of madness to the French villager, the sight of all hands brushing teeth with the horse-trough water and spitting foam on the cobbles must have convinced him."

The gripes of the doughboys when they got to the frontline trenches were about the same as enlisted men's complaints in any and all wars: the weather, which seemed to be either rainy or cold and with mud ever present; the irregularity and slowness of the mail, which was torturous to homesick young men; the Army's inscrutable ways of operating; the unhappy realization that they were there to kill human beings and destroy things; the gripping fear of death or mutilation; the ear-shattering noises of battle as a thousand or more big guns challenged each other; the many, different, ugly smells of battle and its aftermath from the rotting stench of corpses to the foul body odors of the buddy sleeping nearby who had not bathed in a week; and the surprisingly deep hatred and contempt that can fester within enlisted men toward officers. One soldier commented later: "This great adventure stuff was all right, but it did not make you feel any less like a stranded orphan child far away in Lorraine. However, play the game and don't fail to salute your superior officer. He salutes his superior, who salutes Pershing, who salutes the President whom you elected to give you orders in time of war."

France became the testing ground of the reformers' use of the training camps in America to imbue the recruits with progressive and middle-class values, and generally they were satisfied with the doughboys' conduct. They had feared that the temptations of France, especially of Paris, would corrupt the soldiers' morals. Actually, the dangers of Paris were no greater than those of New Orleans or a score of other American cities, but Fosdick's Commission on Training Camp Activities, of course, could not threaten to remove the AEF from France if Premier Clemenceau refused to close the Parisian brothels. The Army could and did, however, make a determined effort to keep the Yanks out of the whorehouses and in camp at night. It sent them to special leave areas where recreation was carefully planned, and it enforced a rigid system of prophylaxis. These measures resulted in a rate of venereal disease far below that of the American civilian population in 1918.

Furthermore, few soldiers seemed to find permanently attractive what were assumed to be French standards of sexual promiscuity. The impact of Army life and of the dramatic separation from America was great, but it did not take the form of a conscious rejection of American virtues in favor of others. The provincialism and naiveté of the bulk of the enlisted men resulted in basically simple reactions to their overseas experiences. They disliked the Army, but most also disliked France, at least in comparison to America. The country and the language were strange. That France was associated with the Army and the war was enough to rob it of much of its charm for tired, homesick doughboys.

Yet the soldiers had gone to war optimistic and returned home confident, even cocky. Their officers had trained them for open, aggressive warfare, and they usually were able to fight their kind of war—offensive actions. In addition, thanks largely to Pershing's stubbornness, they fought in the war's last stage as a distinctive American force.

The doughboys did not constitute the vanguard of the revolution in mores and morals that occurred in America during the twenties. There was disgust with European bickering, and there was suspicion of Wilsonian idealism. Most of the gifted antiwar authors who were alienated from middle-class life and led the way into the Jazz Age were too young to have served in World War I. The enlisted men of the AEF returned home to join the American Legion, which was created in France to combat a post-armistice letdown in morale, and the chronicler of the Yanks' lives in the 1920s was most likely Sinclair Lewis. The doughboys became the George Babbitts of that era, not the "flaming youth" of F. Scott Fitzgerald.

As for the value of the citizen-soldiers of the AEF, the forty-three American divisions that fought in the final battles of the war did not constitute a polished military machine by any means. Often soldiers went into battle without much skill even in Pershing's sine qua non, marksmanship; and many of them did not have the four months' training that the War Department prescribed. In their memoirs, German officers often took a condescending attitude toward the American soldiers' performances. Field Marshal von Hindenburg, for instance, said that the American troops "were not yet quite up to the level of modern requirements in a purely military sense." It is true that the American casualties were disproportionately high for the time they were engaged, in part because the American soldiers were not battle-wise like the French, British, and Germans and made some costly amateurish mistakes. On the other hand, American casualties were high also because the AEF displayed an aggressiveness and a confidence the European forces had lost by the time the United States entered the war.

The Germans may have denigrated the abilities of the doughboys in their postwar writings, but the evidence from their afteraction battlefield reports from Belleau Wood onward betray their real attitudes. As Yanks began to arrive in huge numbers in the summer of 1918, German field commanders found the news highly disturbing. When Americans in combat showed strength and élan despite their lack of a strong national martial tradition and despite their diverse ethnic backgrounds, the Germans did not know what to make of it, so contrary was the doughboys' overall performance to what Kaiser Wilhelm's propaganda pronouncements had predicted. The Americans' dash and confidence exhibited in the St. Mihiel and Meuse-Argonne offensives upset German calculations so badly the high command went into a despondency from which it never emerged, except to importune the civil government to sue for peace.

The American citizen-soldiers in France thoroughly erased the early misgivings of their own conservative and hard-driving AEF commander. Pershing wrote Baker in July 1918: "The fact is that our men are far and away superior to the tired Europeans. High officers of the Allies have often dropped derogatory remarks." Pershing told the Allies "in rather forcible language, that we had now been patronized as long as we would stand for it, and I wished to hear no more of that sort of nonsense."

The Meuse-Argonne campaign of September–November 1918 was the greatest operation fought by the United States Army up to that time, involving the most men and casualties. Afterward Pershing, as dedicated a professional soldier as this nation ever produced, was high in praise of his "partially trained troops" who "prosecuted" the battle "with an unselfish and heroic spirit of courage and fortitude which demanded eventual victory." The pride felt by Pershing and other high-ranking regular officers in the victorious doughboys was to affect profoundly and favorably the military establishment's postwar attitude toward the role of the citizen-soldier. The Army's new esteem for such nonregular troops would be fortunate two decades hence, for citizen-soldiers would prove even more valuable in the Second World War.

Because of the contributions in 1917–1919 of American women and African-American soldiers in Europe, both groups would be given much larger participation overseas in the Second World War. An estimated 25,000 American women served abroad during the World War I period. Of these, 10,000 served in the Army and Navy Nurse corps, often working in dangerous, difficult situations. One nurse described an underground, improvised hospital: "I have not seen daylight for eight days now and the stench in this cave is pretty bad: no air, artificial light, and the cots are so close together you can just get between them. Side by side I have Americans, English, Scotch, Irish, and French, and apart in the corners are Boche. They have to watch each other die."

American women also served overseas in other capacities with the Army and American medical, welfare, and relief agencies. Many relieved AEF males for combat duty, functioning as telephone and telegraph operators, secretaries and clerks, dietitians, cooks, assistants in relief and reclamation projects, and hospital aides. Thousands more worked for the welfare and recreation of the soldiers under the auspices of the Red Cross, YMCA, Salvation Army, and religious organizations. Still others served with foreign relief, entertainment, and medical agencies.

The AEF included 200,000 African Americans in its ranks in France and England, with another 170,000 on stateside duty. Over 160,000 of the African Americans in the AEF were assigned to the Services of Supply, largely as manual laborers at ports and rear-area supply depots. Most of those assigned to combat were concentrated in the 92nd and 93rd divisions, the four regiments of the latter serving in French sectors. Perhaps the most famous of these was the 369th Infantry Regiment, or "Men of Bronze," which spent 191 days in combat attached to the French Army. Many American white troops were reluctant to have black soldiers on their flanks, accepting erroneous rumors that blacks were unreliable in combat. Both of the largely African-American divisions, however, conducted themselves well in comparison to white AEF units under comparable battle conditions. Throughout their tours of duty in Europe, the stigmas of racism and segregation dogged the African-American soldiers: physical abuse and verbal harassment, few chances for promotion, inferior rations and medical services, and other clear signals of their unequal status. When they returned home, they often were denied celebrations in their honor and faced continuing segregation, job discrimination, and sometimes violence despite their patriotic service. Both women and blacks glimpsed many opportunities on the horizon during the Great War, but little did they realize how distant that horizon actually was.

CHAPTER THREE

Nineteen Months of Progress on the Home Front

In spite of the short time the American home front existed, developments in the period 1917–1918 influenced American economic, social, and political institutions for years to come. Like the role played by the American Expeditionary Forces, the contribution of the home front in the United States to the war itself is still much debated by historians. In fact, the American military commitment came so late in the Great War that full mobilization of resources in the United States was neither possible nor necessary.

The brief-lived home front did give birth to a surprising number of experiments, especially at the federal level, for organizing a nation at war without resorting to a militarist or overly centralized system of controls. As Wilson had predicted in calling for United States' belligerency, democracy at home was threatened and civil rights limited, but America survived the period of national emergency without establishing a large permanent central bureaucracy with sweeping powers. Instead, innovative programs attempted to mobilize minds, economic production, and manpower. While the wartime system of 1917–1918 produced mixed results, many of its experiments were later replayed and contributed to fighting the Great Depression and the Second World War.

Agencies of War

The organizations created by the government for wartime purposes relied heavily on voluntary efforts and involved both the public and private sectors. One of the more unusual federal organizations was the Council of National Defense, set up in September 1916 under an Army appropriations measure and chaired by Secretary of War Baker. The Council itself consisted of six cabinet secretaries who set and coordinated policy for economic mobilization, while its Advisory Commission oversaw much of the implementation.

Composed of seven respected leaders in different fields, the Advisory Commission was ably headed by Daniel Willard, president of the Baltimore and Ohio Railway, who also functioned as the principal transportation expert. Samuel Gompers, the powerful head of the American Federation of Labor (AFL) since its founding in 1886, chaired the labor committee and promoted workers' concerns while showing a practical approach to management. An immigrant, strong nationalist, and longtime supporter of Wilson, Gompers played a crucial role in the trade unions' cooperation with industry and government during the war.

Another notable member of the commission was Julius Rosenwald, a philanthropist and the head of the booming Sears, Roebuck mail-order business. He oversaw mobilization efforts in the complex area of supplies, particularly clothing for the troops in France, who called him "General Merchandise." Numerous other committees and technical boards assisted the Council of National Defense and its advisors, both national and local. Many of the participants were "dollar-a-year men" who volunteered their services to the federal government, which by law had to pay them at least a nominal fee.

The Council's Munitions Committee was reorganized as the War Industries Board (WIB) and in early 1918 was put under Bernard M. Baruch, the gifted, aggressive head of the Drexel Institute and future advisor to several American presidents. A close friend of Wilson from South Carolina, Baruch was forty-eight when the president chose him to direct an unprecedented federal intervention in the nation's economy. By then Baruch had achieved startling success in his financial ventures, becoming a multimillionaire through shrewd Wall Street speculation and organizing his own highly successful global company in economic development. Democratic party leaders appreciated his generosity, his political advice, and "golden touch."

The War Industries Board continued to regulate munitions, its original charge, besides overseeing industrial growth, allocation of resources, and price-fixing. Under federal direction, one-fourth of civilian production was converted to war production. The WIB wielded enormous powers over economic activities, participating in the operation of private businesses to a degree previously unknown in the country. To acquire more materials for military purposes, the WIB ordered corset makers to stop using metal stays, shoemakers to use less leather, and coffin makers to eliminate brass, bronze, and copper from caskets. The hemlines of women's skirts grew shorter after calls to conserve cloth. In its efforts to reduce waste of labor and materials, the WIB persuaded manufacturers to standardize production wherever possible, reducing, for example, the numbers of different plow sizes, typewriter ribbon colors, and styles of baby carriages made in the United States.

Baruch's board was largely successful, though charged with more responsibilities than it could sometimes manage. The failure to supply American aircraft, machine guns, and field artillery to Pershing's troops resulted in criticism of the WIB, although the War and Navy departments actually controlled the allocation of these weapons. Because of the shortages, American forces in Europe had to obtain most of these items from the British and French governments.

After the war, Baruch accompanied the president to the peace conference as his economic adviser and served on several Allied committees. In late 1919 when several of Wilson's closest confidants had lost favor with the president, Baruch retained his privileged status at the White House. He continued to counsel White

House occupants, including Republicans, until his death in 1965, though his principal exercise of public power was as Wilson's WIB chairman. He never held an elective post.

One of the truly crucial wartime agencies was the Railroad Administration, which was headed by Secretary of the Treasury William G. McAdoo, an excellent, hardworking administrator. Tall and thin, with intense, deep-set eyes, McAdoo was married to Wilson's daughter Eleanor. He threw his energies into a number of important wartime roles. At a time when motor vehicles and highways were in their infancy, the railways were vital to the transportation of strategic raw materials, military manufactures, and troops. McAdoo merged the lines of nearly 3,000 companies into one single nationwide system for the duration of the war. The operation of the giant system was shared by the federal government and organized labor with the railroad firms. Priorities and allocations for military freight and traffic were rigidly protected. Also placed under wartime federal regulation were telephone and telegraph companies, in which management and labor generally cooperated.

Problems inevitably arose because the transportation and communications services could not meet the expanded needs of 4 million uniformed personnel, much less those of the millions of civilians moving to new jobs spawned by the war. Related to the rail difficulties were the shortages in petroleum and coal faced by the Fuel Administration. During the unusually severe winter of 1917–1918, snarled rail lines left many homes and businesses dangerously lacking in fuel, while coal cars lay still in congested yards and coal barges were ice-bound on major river arteries and the Great Lakes. Many factories temporarily shut their doors during the fuel crisis. At other times during the war, the need to conserve fuel forced heatless days, lightless nights, shorter hours for businesses, and gasolineless Sundays. In the spring of 1918 the country adopted daylight savings time to conserve energy during the war.

Probably the most impressive achievements in economic mobilization were wrought by the Food Administration under the direction of Herbert C. Hoover. By any measure, Wilson's selection of Hoover ranks among the president's most judicious appointments. Like Baruch, Hoover acquired early wealth and worldwide distinction in his professional field, which was mining engineering. Orphaned at an early age and reared in Quaker communities, Hoover excelled at organizing relief programs, which often focused on the needs of hungry children. In the fall of 1914, Hoover himself initiated an ambitious effort to feed starving civilians in areas of Belgium and France occupied by German troops. His humanitarian agency saved millions of people from malnutrition.

Assuming control of the Food Administration in 1917, Hoover's charge was to provide food for needy Allied nations as well as for American Army and Navy units in the European war zone. Relying on the patriotism of American consumers and producers, Hoover used voluntary rather than coercive methods to increase the amount of food available to send to Europe. Especially needed for export were meat, fat, sugar, and wheat. Working closely with farmers, middlemen, grocers, and agricultural associations, he encouraged increases in production and the allocation of nonperishable foodstuffs for transport overseas. Subsidies to farmers resulted in the dramatic expansion of many crops, particularly wheat.

In his complementary effort to reduce civilian food consumption, Hoover rejected the option of rationing, campaigning instead for voluntary self-sacrifice. One agency poster entitled "Blood or Bread" made the argument: "Others are giving their blood. You will shorten the war—save life if you eat only what you need and waste nothing." The public enthusiastically adopted such official slogans as "Food will win the war." Americans planted vegetable "war gardens" in their yards and, in the case of urban dwellers, in vacant lots. They responded to Hoover's appeals for wheatless Mondays, meatless Tuesdays, and porkless Saturdays. The Food Administration urged Americans to "save" and "serve the cause of freedom" by substituting corn for wheat, fish and beans for meat, and syrups for sugar. Food conservation, or "Hooverizing," as it was popularly known, was highly successful. Hoover's managerial genius and his deep commitment to voluntarism enabled the United States to feed civilians and soldiers both at home and abroad. After the war Hoover successfully ran a massive relief program in Europe, a feat he repeated following the Second World War. Ironically, as president, Hoover failed in attempts to alleviate suffering due to malnutrition in his own country during the Great Depression.

Surely the longest legacy of the wartime agencies established for the mobilization of resources was the War Finance Corporation (WFC), which was promoted by McAdoo. By providing liberal government credit, it assisted the corporations most vital to the war effort in both conversion to military needs and later reconversion to civilian functions. Targeting indispensable war industries and financial institutions, the WFC could issue up to $3 billion in bonds. Though the WFC was not formed until April 1918, too late to affect the Great War, it gave a much-needed boost to the most important firms that were pacing the nation's war output. During the Great Depression, the WFC was revived and revised as the Reconstruction Finance Corporation.

As in the cases of manpower and economic mobilization, the financing of the war depended heavily on cooperation and coordination among the public sector, private associations, and individuals. Including loans to the Allies, the United States' war expenses totaled over $31 billion from April 1917 through April 1919—a cost far greater than in any previous American conflict. One-third of the financial burden was covered by taxes, especially the federal income tax system authorized by the Sixteenth Amendment in 1913. According to wartime legislation, individuals with a taxable minimum income of $1,000 paid 2 percent in taxes; those with the highest incomes paid 65 percent. Rates for corporations also increased sharply. The new rules forced many Americans to pay income taxes for the first time, but the revenues produced formed an indispensable part of the American financing of the war.

In contrast to previous American wars, when wealthy men and large businesses funded most government drives, McAdoo decided that the Liberty Loans and Victory Loans of 1917–1919 would target individual purchasers. According to him, "we went direct to the people" and "capitalized the profound impulse called patriotism." In amazingly successful drives, the goals for bond sales were more than met. Businesses, schools, churches, community organizations, and film stars such as Mary Pickford and Douglas Fairbanks participated in well-publicized campaigns to encourage the purchase of war bonds. Widely distributed posters urged Americans to "Beat Back the Hun with Liberty Bonds" and to buy bonds "That Liberty Shall Not Perish." With the cheapest bonds priced at fifty dollars, people of many income levels supported the drives. In gaining a financial stake in the war effort, many were caught up in a momentum that made them more likely to buy more bonds in succeeding drives. The government also sold War Savings Certificates for five dollars and Thrift Stamps for twenty-five cents, which were often bought by school children who wanted to "Lick a Stamp and Lick the Kaiser."

Life on the Home Front

Affluence and inflation, the strange bedfellows of war periods in American history, began well before the formal entry of the United States into the hostilities in Europe. As European demands for war-related materials and loans from the United States escalated, and the materiel needs of the American military establishment grew, the nation found itself suddenly transformed from a debtor to a creditor in its world trade relations. This change, as well as the government's award of unbelievably lucrative contracts to major defense contractors, precipitated a boom era that affected virtually every section of the country and nearly all fields of work. Farmers whose products were especially needed by the Allies saw their profits rise quickly. While prosperity was not uniform in agriculture, it was common among businessmen. In some commercial areas, particularly defense-related industries, war profiteering became blatant. The huge cantonments quickly erected, mainly in the South, brought unbelievable profits to the training camps' builders and suppliers, along with immediate affluence to retail businesses in nearby communities. The number of new "war millionaires" increased sharply.

Wartime inflation was never brought under satisfactory control, mainly because the people would not have tolerated the government's arbitrary regulation of wages and prices. Although deeply anxious about inflation's impact on various aspects of the war effort, Wilson restricted his efforts to suasion and repeated pressures on business leaders to tighten voluntarily their prices and wage rates. He also set up the National War Labor Board and the War Labor Policies Board to resolve labor's grievances.

For the duration of the war, the American Federation of Labor, under Gompers's leadership, worked fairly well with the federal government and employers in accepting rising pay levels and not pushing for unreasonably higher ones. With the demand for labor high, some union leaders opposed Gompers' willingness to cooperate in wartime in exchange for long-term advances for labor. In spite of their dissatisfaction, however, union membership grew with the increase of people in the labor force. As it turned out, wartime cooperation marked a tentative and brief truce between labor and management. Troubled relations had preceded America's entry into the war and erupted, after the armistice, into a volatile period of labor violence.

At the same time that defense industries expanded, many men left their jobs to enter the armed forces, and immigration nearly halted. As the shortage of labor intensified, opportunities opened for new groups to enter the workforce. During the war years, the number of women with paying jobs grew to 1.5 million in the United States. Many other women carried out volunteer work or served abroad for the war effort. Although the National War Labor Board generally endorsed the principle that women who performed jobs usually held by men should receive "equal pay for equal work," this did not happen often. In addition to clerical and industrial work, women assumed such visible occupations as streetcar conductors, traffic police, and mail carriers. To free more men to go overseas, the Navy permitted women to enlist as female yeomen, whose primary duties were clerical and confined to American locations. The Army and Marines also accepted women. While the war allowed women more job opportunities, few of these continued after the war when the troops returned to civilian life. Military service for most women ended, along with many factory jobs and other wartime positions.

Nonetheless, as more women entered the workforce for the first time, other women continued their campaign for suffrage. The more militant groups such as the National Woman's Party, led by Alice Paul, forcefully pressured the government to grant women the right to vote. Throughout the war groups of suffragists, including many socially prominent women, picketed the White House each day, carrying banners calling the president "Kaiser Wilson" and burning him in effigy. At times the Washington police used physical force to arrest the picketers, who were convicted of disturbing the peace and then sentenced to the workhouse for refusing to pay their fines. The president pardoned some protesters, while others served terms of up to six months. Authorities moved the most recalcitrant women to solitary confinement and force-fed those on hunger strikes. One jailed group announced to the local commissioners: "As political prisoners, we, the undersigned, refuse to work while in prison" and should receive "the rights due political prisoners."

While some women's groups sought to achieve their goals by openly challenging the government, other organizations used different tactics. By participating in public patriotic activities, Carrie Chapman Catt and other prominent suffragists influenced much of the general public, as well as Washington leaders, to adopt a more tolerant view of a proposal for a woman's suffrage amendment. Catt, who headed the National American Woman Suffrage Association, joined the Women's Committee of the Council of National Defense and urged American women to support the war by selling bonds, rolling bandages, conserving food, and marching in parades. To members of her organization who wanted to focus either on war work or on the suffrage crusade, Catt said, "We must do both." Opponents of suffrage complained that leaders like Catt volunteered to help the war effort only in exchange for the right to vote.

In January 1918 the House of Representatives approved the woman's suffrage amendment. Wilson endorsed it on the eve of the congressional elections that November, proclaiming to the nation: "We have made partners of the women in this war. Shall we admit them only to a partnership of suffering and sacrifice and toil and not to a partnership of privilege and right?" Although it was not ratified until 1920, the Nineteenth Amendment became reality, in part, because of wartime conditions.

The labor shortage that opened opportunities to women also made a dramatic impact on African Americans. Hundreds of thousands of blacks left poverty-stricken rural environments in the South to move to higher-paying jobs and more promising futures in large metropolitan centers such as Chicago, Detroit, St. Louis, Philadelphia, New York, and Houston. Northern job recruiters pledged wages higher than the fifty to seventy-five cents paid daily by many Southern employers. The huge migration into areas previously dominated by whites, however, culminated in dozens of bloody race riots during and immediately after the war. Continuing issues such as segregation and racial injustice contributed to clashes. Ninety-six African Americans were lynched across the country in 1917–1918.

Draft practices reinforced the segregation of blacks and also led to violence, especially in large cities where there were so many other grievances. While the same local draft boards registered and classified both blacks and whites, eligible blacks were inducted separately. The boards, usually made up of whites, drafted a higher percentage of the registered blacks than of whites, often by giving whites more exemptions for having families, disabilities, or essential occupations.

In spite of the obstacles blocking them from equal citizenship, many blacks served in the armed forces or fully supported the war effort at home. Civil rights organizations, however, differed concerning their proper relationship with the government during wartime. As occurred in the woman's suffrage movement, some leaders saw wartime as an opportunity to demonstrate their patriotism and good citizenship, which could lead to the achievement of equal rights. In July 1918, W. E. B. Du Bois, the influential black leader, told black Americans: "Let us not hesitate. Let us, while the war lasts, forget our special grievances and close ranks shoulder to shoulder with our white fellow citizens" in "fighting for democracy." Countering Du Bois were activists such as J. E. Mitchell, editor of the *St. Louis Argus,* who argued that blacks should not fight for the cause of democracy abroad until they had achieved full rights at home: "Now is the time to protest. Now is the time to complain. Now is the time to contend for legal rights that are being denied us, and now is the time to let the world know that we are not satisfied." After the war ended, Du Bois resumed his pressure on the government for racial justice, writing: "We return. We return from fighting. We return fighting."

The great African-American migration from rural to urban areas was only one aspect of the massive demographic changes that occurred during wartime. As the country rapidly mobilized, the number of workers needed to administer the new federal programs grew rapidly, ranging from clerical workers to dollar-a-year officials. To accommodate the new agencies in Washington, the government erected "tempos," or temporary office buildings, along the Mall near the Smithsonian buildings. It later added spartan barracks for clerks between Union Station and the Senate Office Building. Housing in Washington became so scarce that in order to fill their jobs some newcomers reportedly had to "travel back and forth on night trains" in order to have a place to sleep.

The population in areas near defense-related industries also expanded dramatically. New workers faced severe housing shortages and excessive rents, resulting in such situations as ten workers occupying one room and sleeping in shifts. Communities that solicited workers without planning for their housing were criticized by a federal official for behaving as if "laborers came along like tortoises, with their homes on their backs." In perhaps the largest population change of all, more than 4 million men and women left their homes and entered the armed forces. Most spent at least part of their military service in crowded training camps hastily erected across the country.

The personal needs of the servicemen at home and abroad were met by dedicated service organizations in perhaps the zenith of voluntarism and associationalism during the war. The American Red Cross operated the largest of such programs, using the time and talents of thousands of volunteers to relieve human suffering. In the United States the Red Cross improved sanitary conditions in the areas adjoining the training facilities and assisted the poor or ill families of troops. Working in close cooperation with the military authorities, it offered a wide range of health, welfare, and educational services for the troops in America and abroad. It furnished servicemen with personal articles, hot meals, and beverages. In military hospitals its workers nursed, counseled, wrote letters for patients, and otherwise helped recuperating soldiers, in addition to working with civilian relief efforts abroad.

Also active in assistance and relief were the Young Men's Christian Association (YMCA), the Salvation Army, the War Camp Community Service, the American Library Association, the Jewish Welfare Board, the National Catholic War Council, and other organizations representing Protestant churches. The YMCA built "Y-huts" to house recreational activities, which included hosting dances, showing motion pictures, providing hot showers, and serving food. Although these agencies did much to help troops in stateside bases and on the Western Front, some drew criticism, especially the "Y", for charging fees for cigarettes and other items.

Many in the AEF favored the Salvation Army, which offered them free fresh doughnuts and coffee and also mended soldiers' clothes as part of the "Soup, Soap, and Salvation" campaign. Their workers, usually husband-and-wife teams, had performed relief work in American slums and empathized with the soldiers' plights, whether at Camp Shelby, Mississippi, or in the trenches near St. Mihiel, France. In all, the work of the private service organizations was essential in meeting the personal needs and maintaining the common morale of the fighting forces. As in other aspects of the war, the federal government depended heavily on volunteer associations even in the case of its most powerful instrument, its military establishment.

Although American volunteers contributed significantly to the war effort, their enthusiastic support also had darker aspects. Like the holy crusades of the past, the patriotic excitement sometimes turned to war hysteria and persecution of those who dissented from what was perceived as the majority opinion. Socialists, pacifists, members of radical labor groups, and German Americans were particularly targeted by "patriotic" zealots, from the community level to Capitol Hill. While many of the persecuted groups

Left: President Woodrow Wilson. Reproduced courtesy of the George C. Marshall Research Library.

Below: Secretary of War Newton D. Baker (in blindfold) draws a number in the nation's first large-scale conscription. U.S. Army Signal Corps photograph. Reproduced courtesy of the George C. Marshall Research Library.

Opposite top: British Field Marshal Douglas Haig (left) and American General John J. Pershing. Reproduced courtesy of the George C. Marshall Research Library.

Opposite bottom: French and American soldiers join in a toast, April 1918. Courtesy of the National Archives.

Below: American doughboys and British WAACs behind the lines, June 27, 1918. Courtesy of the National Archives.

CAN
Vegetables
Fruit AND
the Kaiser too

Tomatoes

Peas

Kaiser Brand
Unsweetened

Write for Free Book to
National War Garden Commission
WASHINGTON, D.C.

Charles Lathrop Pack - President   P.S. Ridsdale - Secretary

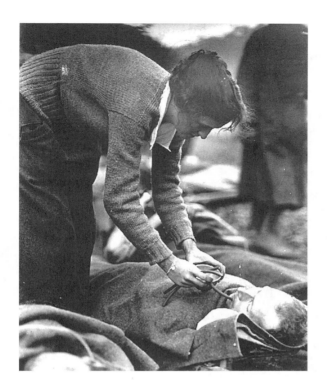

*Above: 166th infantry soldier being fed by a nurse at a hospital in
Soilly in the Meuse region. Courtesy of the National Archives.*

*Opposite top: Meuse-Argonne Offensive, September 1918. U.S.
Army Signal Corps photograph. Reproduced courtesy of the
George C. Marshall Research Library.*

Opposite bottom: Poster by J. Paul Verrees, Can Vegetables, Fruit
and the Kaiser, Too, *ca., 1917. Courtesy of the Art Collection,
Harry Ransom Humanities Research Center, The University of
Texas at Austin.*

Above: Actress Theda Bara speaks in support of the fourth Liberty Loan Drive. Courtesy of the National Archives.

Left: Poster by Howard Chandler Christy, Americans All, *1919. Courtesy of Museum of the City of New York, gift of John W. Campbell.*

Opposite top: At the Paris Peace Conference, 1919 (left to right) British Prime Minister David Lloyd George, Italian Premier Vittorio Orlando, French Premier Georges Clemenceau, and American President Woodrow Wilson. U.S. Army Signal Corps photograph. Reproduced courtesy of the George C. Marshall Research Library.

Opposite bottom: African-American soldiers returning to New York, 1919. Courtesy of the National Archives.

"Over the top." U.S. Army Signal Corps photo. Courtesy of George C. Marshall Research Library, Lexington, Virginia.

had opposed American participation in the Great War, they did not necessarily want the Central powers to win. But their criticism of war in general, capitalism, or violations of civil rights in the name of wartime exigency drew public ire and accusations of disloyalty or worse.

Congress, in a fervor of patriotic zeal that crossed party lines, passed legislation to suppress the spread of alleged disloyalty and to maintain the public image of remarkable national unity behind the war effort. The Espionage Act of June 1917 punished violators with prison sentences of up to twenty years and fines of $10,000. It covered such loosely defined crimes as encouraging others to be disloyal, aiding the enemy, refusing to serve in the military, and sending "treasonable" materials through the mail. This last part was energetically enforced by the Postmaster General, who banned the distribution of socialist, pro-Irish, and other radical publications. The Supreme Court later upheld the Espionage Act in a decision written by Oliver Wendell Holmes, Jr., who found that certain circumstances could present "a clear and present danger." He wrote further that "when a nation is at war," freedom of speech could be limited.

Expanding the "crimes of disloyalty," the Sedition Act of May 1918 prohibited "disloyal, profane, scurrilous, or abusive language" about the government, the flag, the Constitution, or the armed forces. Under a measure passed near the end of the war, the secretary of labor could bypass the jury-trial system and deport aliens accused of destroying government property, advocating the forcible overthrow of the government, or belonging to organizations that allegedly supported such positions.

As a result of these laws, Socialist leader Eugene V. Debs received a prison sentence for telling his followers that they did not deserve to be "cannon fodder." One prominent woman went to prison for ten years for stating that she opposed the war because "the government is for the profiteers." Many others, including pacifists with long-held views, were also convicted.

One target of both government and private citizens was the radical Industrial Workers of the World (IWW), or "Wobblies," whose labor strikes and opposition to the war gained it influence with many poor, migratory workers. Members of the IWW, also derisively called "I Won't Work" or "Imperial Wilhelm's Warriors," were harassed, tarred and feathered, and even lynched by bands of vigilantes. The government accused the IWW of crimes under the Espionage and Sedition acts, sending more than one hundred Wobblies to prison. Among those charged was their leader, William D. Haywood, who escaped and fled to Russia.

Pressure to stamp out dissent spread through the country at many levels. The Wisconsin legislature censured its own Senator Robert La Follette for opposing American participation in the war, and the U.S. Senate considered his expulsion, although he supported later legislation for conducting the war. (By 1924 he had regained public respect, making a strong showing as a Progressive candidate for president.)

To show their patriotism many states proclaimed English to be their official language. The governor of Iowa banned the use of other languages in schools, in public speeches, and in "conversation in public places, or trains, or over the telephone." He further ordered that religious services be conducted in English and instructed speakers of other languages to worship at home. Many communities prohibited the teaching of German and burned library books written by German authors or in German. Streets, public buildings, and even entire towns with Germanic names were renamed. Some military volunteers altered their family names from "Schmitt" to "Smith" to avoid rejection, ridicule, or ostracism. In the height of renouncing all things German, some Americans changed "sauerkraut" to "liberty cabbage," "dachshund" to "liberty dog," and "German measles" to "liberty measles."

Vigilantes often ostracized or openly persecuted people who had foreign-sounding names, who expressed "disloyal" views about the government, or who appeared suspicious in some way. In Colorado supranationalists badly beat a man confined to a wheelchair when he simply criticized President Wilson for leading the nation into an unnecessary war. Local groups nailed yellow cards to houses of those who refused to purchase war bonds. Private volunteer groups also worked with the Justice Department to carry out "slacker raids," in which they rounded up men who appeared to be of draft age from theaters, train stations, and ballparks. Draft boards then investigated the suspected draft evaders, often detaining them for weeks.

Contributing to the public's attitudes toward the war was one of the most controversial agencies established by Wilson. Set up in April 1917, the Committee on Public Information (CPI) was headed by a talented, if sometimes erratic and sensation-minded, journalist named George Creel, who was personally very close to the president. The CPI included the secretaries of the State, War, and Navy departments, but Creel held the principal responsibility for running what Baker called "the whole business of mobilizing the mind of the world." As did the heads of other wartime agencies, Creel relied heavily on voluntarism, from the bankers and clergymen who conveyed his ideas to the newspapers that practiced self-censorship.

The CPI focused on "the war will" of the American people through a massive propaganda campaign of news releases, pamphlets, films, and speeches. Creel recruited well-known illustrators including N. C. Wyeth and James Montgomery Flagg to design posters which he displayed on billboards, walls, barns, and other structures in a "battle of the fences." Some 75,000 people volunteered to give brief patriotic talks on such topics as war bonds, draft registration, food conservation, and "Maintaining Morals and Morale." These "Four Minute Men" often spoke in motion-picture theaters while the silent film reels were being changed; they also led groups in singing "Keep the Home Fires Burning" and "The Star Spangled Banner." Others spoke at schools, civic meetings, and various public gatherings.

The CPI championed the righteousness of the Allied cause while depicting the Germans as nefarious, warlike peoples descended from barbarians. After the war some of the volunteers regretted their participation in the ethnic smearing and truth-bending that sometimes occurred. Creel and the CPI helped to build the wartime spirit of national unity, but they also contributed to the widespread intolerance of dissent across the country.

Due in part to the government's efforts, Americans attending public places of entertainment received frequent allusions to the war in Europe. Moviegoers could watch CPI-originated newsreels and films like *Pershing's Crusaders* or they could view commercially produced films concerning the war, such as *To Hell with the Kaiser* and *The Little American*. In the latter film, the character played by Mary Pickford was forced to clean the boots of the autocratic German officer who threatened to rape her. While D. W. Griffith and other members of the young silent-film industry in Hollywood enthusiastically supported the war effort, not all of their films involved the war. Releases in 1917–1918 also included *Rebecca of Sunnybrook Farm* and *Tarzan of the Apes*.

Anti-German sentiment extended to music in many communities, resulting in cancellations of performances by German musicians and the banning of German operas and the music of Beethoven. In general, however, plays and musical performances continued to draw large audiences, including soldiers who received theater discounts to Broadway shows, and the president, who regularly attended vaudeville fare in Washington. Many professional performers raised funds for relief work, spoke at bond rallies, and entertained the troops. It was at this time that the playing of "The Star Spangled Banner," which was not then the national anthem, became a standard part of public events. While all popular music did not concern the war, the best-known songs were George M. Cohan's "Over There" and Irving Berlin's camp song "How I Hate to Get Up in the Morning." Cohan's lyrics, written the day after the U.S. entered the war, reflected the attitudes of many Americans about their impact overseas:

> Over there, over there,
> Send the word, send the word over there,
> That the Yanks are coming, the Yanks are coming,
> The drums rum-tumming everywhere.
> So prepare, say a prayer,
> Send the word, send the word to beware,
> We'll be over, we're coming over,
> And we won't come back till
> It's over over there.

Other songs well liked by soldiers and civilians included "Beautiful K-K-Katy," "Hinky Dinky Parlay-Voo," and "I'm Proud to Be the Mother of a Soldier."

When the United States entered the war, baseball and boxing were popular throughout the country. In 1917 prominent military and governmental leaders appeared as guests of honor at the beginning of professional baseball games, followed by players marching on to the fields holding their bats like rifles on their shoulders. Inductees into the armed services played sports in training camps and learned boxing as an Army training exercise. When *The Stars and Stripes,* the soldiers' newspaper in France, first began to publish in early 1918, it regularly carried reports of sports events in the United States.

As the war progressed and American casualties mounted, however, professional sports came under increasing attacks for enabling healthy men of draft age to remain civilians and earn high salaries, while other Americans entered the armed forces and risked their lives. In protest *The Stars and Stripes* stopped its coverage of American sports and editorialized that a professional athlete who has made "a tidy fortune" now "owes it to his country to do something in return." Under pressure the national baseball leagues shortened their season, cutting salaries accordingly. In the summer of 1918 Secretary Baker announced that professional baseball was not an "essential industry," as team owners had argued, and that players would have to get war jobs or "shoulder guns and fight." Some players took jobs in defense factories; others died on the battlefields of France.

Increasingly throughout the 1917–1918 period, Americans faced daily reminders of their country's involvement in the war. With the signing of the armistice and the release of most soldiers to civilian status, much of the country returned to the familiar conditions desired by so many. While many facets of everyday life were only temporarily altered by the war, other aspects changed permanently.

Progressivism and Politics

American involvement in the war forced Wilson to delay his plans for expanding progressivism at the federal level, much as domestic reforms were curtailed during World War II and the Vietnam conflict. The great reform movement that had wrought significant changes at national, state, and local levels since the turn of the century did not altogether die, but the voices of reformers were more muffled, and their achievements less far-reaching during the First World War and the subsequent decade.

Two reforms that did advance legislatively during the war and became law soon afterward were constitutional amendments concerning prohibition and woman's suffrage. The Eighteenth Amendment banned the "manufacture, sale, or transportation of intoxicating liquors," a goal long sought by the temperance movement. More recent advocates of prohibition had argued that edible grains should not be used to make alcohol while children in Europe starved and that liquor sales should be banned near training camps to protect American soldiers from vice. In the Nineteenth Amendment, women received the right to vote, due in part to the visible roles played by many women during the war. Neither measure had the decisive impact desired by its supporters. National prohibition would be widely ignored or violated, while meaningful advances for women in American politics would be denied for decades. Contemporary suffragists were largely disappointed in the anticlimactic aftermath of the ratification of the Nineteenth Amendment.

Wilson himself had been pessimistic about the amendments' widespread implementation and foresaw a postwar decline in the American people's interest in traditional progressive objectives. During his New Jersey governorship and his first term in the White House, Wilson enjoyed the approval of a majority of progressives, many of whom considered him to be the movement's national leader. But his military interventions in Mexico and the Caribbean, his role in leading the United States into the World War, and his advocacy of international security combined to shatter the support of many progressives. An important part of the progressive movement condemned all wars unless necessary for self-defense and opposed any international organization dominated by the great powers.

During the nineteen months America was actually fighting in the Great War, the major political races of national significance were the congressional elections of November 1918, held shortly before the armistice. In these elections the Democrats lost control of both houses of the new Sixty-sixth Congress, with the Republicans winning a slim majority in the Senate and a larger one in the House. The Democratic president may have been among those contributing to the return to power of the Republicans on Capitol Hill. Since America entered the war, both political parties had touted bipartisanship, while practicing it rather sporadically. Eleven days before the 1918 elections, however, Wilson pleaded with the American people to return a Democratic Congress to power so that he could "continue to be your unembarrassed spokesman in affairs at home and abroad." He warned that European leaders would interpret a Republican victory "as a repudiation of my leadership" and weaken his strength in dealing with them. As for the Republicans, they "have unquestionably been pro-war, but they have been anti-administration" and their leaders "desire not so much to support the President as to control him."

Republicans responded furiously to Wilson's openly partisan appeal. Senator Henry Cabot Lodge retorted that "the President has thrown off the mask" of bipartisanship and that a Republican should be "pretty indignant to be told that he cannot be trusted to take part in the government of his country." The administration's relations with the Republicans were not improved by remarks from Creel, who had earned the nickname "Wilson's press agent" by tirelessly promoting the president as well as the war effort. When asked his evaluation of Congressional support of the war, Creel responded that he had "not been slumming for years."

Wilson's pitch to the voters had been ill-advised, but it surely was not the only cause of the Democrats' defeat. With the Allies' massive Meuse-Argonne offensive pressing forward, hostilities were almost over when the elections took place. Undoubtedly voters were weary of the burdens of heavy taxation and troubled by American casualties, which had grown especially large during the preceding five months. Many felt increasingly uneasy about the prospect of new international commitments in the postwar era. Others rejected Wilson's continuing advocacy of reforms needed at home and abroad.

The shift in course politically in the autumn of 1918 also was consistent with the traditional pattern of congressional elections in years when there was no presidential contest. Moreover, as one historian observes: "The first third of the twentieth century was an era of Republican dominance. The Wilson years constituted an interlude," after which "the country simply returned to its normally Republican condition."

Another factor influencing the 1918 elections was the antiquated sectional demography of the Democratic party, which was still anchored primarily in the South and had only tenuous affinities with large voting groups elsewhere. Democratic hopes in the Midwest and West were severely damaged in August 1918 by Wilson's veto of a farm price bill. With this action he briefly slowed inflation but also seriously hurt wheat prices while allowing cotton prices to remain high. His veto, according to one historian, "was the blade that cleaved the West from the Democratic South" and struck "at the weakest spot in the Democratic coalition." For Wilson, the disappointing political outcome of November 1918 would be only the first of many problems that would beset him in the coming year.

CHAPTER FOUR

The Final Wilson Years

Long before the war in Europe ended, Wilson announced his idealistic war aims and peace program to the nation and the world. Addressing both houses of Congress in January 1918, the president enunciated his Fourteen Points, most of which had been mentioned previously by him or European leaders, but never so eloquently. He told his Capitol Hill listeners: "What we demand in this war . . . is nothing peculiar to ourselves. It is that the world be made fit and safe to live in; and particularly that it be made safe for every peace-loving nation which, like our own, wishes to live its own life, determine its own institutions, be assured of justice and fair dealing by the other peoples of the world as against force and selfish aggression."

The first five of Wilson's Fourteen Points were broad, utopian principles: "open covenants of peace openly arrived at"; freedom of the seas; abolition of international trade barriers; reduction of national armaments; and impartial readjustment of all colonial claims, with consideration of the interests of the colonial peoples. The next eight points dealt with revising the maps of Europe and the Near East to reflect more just national, ethnic demographic lines. The fourteenth point, by far the most important to Wilson, called for the establishment of a general association of nations that would guarantee independence, self-rule, territorial integrity, and security to large and small states alike. This organization was to become the League of Nations.

In subsequent addresses, the president mentioned additional points, although only two suggested new directions. In a February speech to Congress, he remarked that "each part of the final settlement must be based on the essential justice of that particular case" and should try to make "a peace that will be permanent." At Mount Vernon in July he emphasized the objective of destroying "every arbitrary power anywhere that can separately, secretly, and of its single choice disturb the peace of the world," adding that "if it can not be presently destroyed, at least its reduction to virtual impotence."

Reaction to Wilson's Fourteen Points was generally favorable, even by congressmen who would later oppose the president in his call for U.S. membership in the League of Nations. To the *New York Herald Tribune,* his address was "one of the great documents in American history." In Germany civilians and soldiers read a translation of Wilson's words, due to the efforts of Creel's Committee on Public Information, which printed the presidential speech and distributed the leaflets by plane behind enemy lines. Wilson's Fourteen Points were printed in newspapers around the world, even in Russia, where Lenin was said to consider them "a great step toward the peace of the world." Acclaim for the Fourteen Points was not universal; in France, Clemenceau reportedly responded: "The Good Lord had only ten!"

Kaiser Wilhelm's government subsequently requested peace on the basis of Wilson's Fourteen Points and the points added in his "subsequent addresses." Germany and its coalition partners hoped their appeal to Wilson's principles might lead to a softer, negotiated peace, as opposed to the vindictive conditions the Allies sought to impose. Instead, the Allies interpreted the collapse of the Central powers in the fall of 1918 as a victory that did not require them to accept a "peace by compromise and negotiation."

In spite of Wilson's noble efforts to direct the postwar settlements onto a higher plane, the conditions in the major Allied countries and on the battlefronts of Europe dictated the harsh peace that provided the seedbed for war again within two decades.

Retreat from Global Responsibility

By the time of the armistice on November 11, 1918, President Wilson was virtually obsessed with the crusade he intended to lead personally at the upcoming Paris Peace Conference, which was to set forth the terms of peace for Germany and to formulate the charter for the League of Nations. He wanted to act as the broker among the vengeance-minded Allied leaders in obtaining a fairer, more generous peace settlement than most of them desired. He also wanted to create an effective international organization, led by the United States, to ensure a postwar world that would be peaceful, free, and no longer handicapped by secret treaties and balance-of-power considerations.

When Wilson traveled to Paris in mid-December, however, several factors severely limited his chances of success. In November, the American voters had dealt him a major setback by repudiating his public campaign to elect Democratic majorities in both houses. His partisan maneuver renewed the vigor of the Republicans, who, after largely supporting the administration during the hostilities, won control of the Senate and House. Their opposition to Wilson's leadership of the peace process was already mounting when he addressed Congress in early December: The Republicans in the audience were "sullen and quiet," according to Josephus Daniels, who described their behavior toward Wilson as "churlish."

The president stumbled also in naming his commission to the treaty conference. As expected, he selected his close advisor House, as well as Secretary of State Lansing and General Tasker H. Bliss, but then added only one Republican, diplomat Henry White, who was not influential in the high circles of his party. Through his selection he had ignored powerful Republican leaders, notably Lodge, who would soon head the Senate Foreign Relations Committee. The president also had upset some of his own Democratic legislative backers by not including a single member of Congress on his peace commission.

Furthermore, Wilson's decision to head the commission himself evoked widespread disapproval among both supporters and adversaries. Traditionally American presidents had not traveled to Europe while in office and had used emissaries to carry out foreign negotiations. *New York World* editor Frank Cobb strongly protested Wilson's plan: "In Washington, President Wilson has the ear of the whole world. It is a commanding position. . . . One of his strongest weapons in his conflict is the very mystery and uncertainty that attach to him while he remains in Washington." Cobb continued that, by sitting down with European leaders, Wilson would lose "all the power that comes from distance and detachment" and become "merely a negotiator dealing with other negotiators." The secretary of state, who was to disagree with the president on other issues, tried without success to persuade him to reconsider, convinced that Wilson was "making one of the greatest mistakes of his career." Initially opposed as well was the French premier, who later favored the president's decision in the belief, according to one observer, that "it will pull Wilson down from his high pedestal." Lodge thought the trip inadvisable but did not object, remarking that "when a political situation is entirely favorable it is not wise to meddle with it."

After a voyage on the *George Washington,* Wilson received a tumultuous welcome in Paris. To the second Mrs. Wilson, "every inch" of the city seemed "covered with cheering, shouting humanity" as the president and his French hosts rode in horse-drawn carriages through the Arc de Triomphe and "flowers rained upon us until we were nearly buried." Similar crowds cheered the president as he traveled through Europe during the month before the conference was to convene. On these journeys he met with dignitaries but also publicly campaigned for his Fourteen Points, angering several Allied officials by appealing directly to their citizens. In at least one case, Italian officials dispersed the crowds before the president could speak to them, "a gross discourtesy" that left him "fairly blazing with anger," according to his wife. She wrote that the Italian "Government, seeing the outpouring of the people, and especially the soldiers, feared that if the President addressed them he would say something which would enlist their support for his Fourteen Points," that many Allied leaders wanted to disavow. Actually, many of Wilson's audiences, while enthusiastically greeting him, felt even more vindictive toward the Central powers than did their heads of state.

On the eve of the peace conference, Wilson's high visibility and his personal advocacy of his Fourteen Points sparked unrealistic hopes in many parts of the world. Downtrodden peoples in many areas believed that the president could secure for them freedom, democracy, and prosperity. Many Germans viewed him as a protector against an unjust peace treaty, while peasants in far-off Korea, hoping for American intervention there, revolted in vain against ruthless Japanese rule.

When the Paris Peace Conference convened in mid-January 1919, thirty-two Allied and "associated" powers were represented. Few plenary sessions met that winter and spring, as national commissions of experts researched and drafted most of the treaty provisions on boundaries, economic stipulations, and other matters. Wilson's group, called "The Inquiry," consisted mainly of specialists from universities and the State Department. At first the executive leadership of the conference was in the hands of the Council of Ten, composed of the heads of state and foreign ministers of France, Britain, the United States, Italy, and Japan. By late March this body was reduced to the Council of Three, consisting of the dominant leaders—Prime Minister David Lloyd George of the United Kingdom, Clemenceau of France, and Wilson.

The eldest of the three was Clemenceau, aged seventy-seven, known for his biting wit and his relentless pressure for punishing Germany. He made a "lasting impression" on House: "Squat of figure, with massive head, penetrating eyes, wide apart and clouded by heavy, irregular eyebrows, overhanging mustache, high cheekbones, he presents with his eternal skullcap and suede gloves a gnome-like appearance. As he used to sit, hour after hour, presiding over conferences, with eyes half closed, his face was a masque. But behind it burned unquenchable fires." According to

Lloyd George, Clemenceau and Wilson did not "understand the
other's best qualities. When Wilson talks idealism, Clemenceau
wonders what he means." An American remarked that, in spite of
their differences, the two made "it seem as if they were on the
closest terms."

Lloyd George had recently won reelection by promising his
voters a harsh peace, reportedly pledging to "squeeze the German
orange until the pips squeak." To an American observer, "Lloyd
George is really the best fun of these conferences; very alert, not
knowing much about things in exact terms; passing comments in a
loud undertone without cessation, regardless of whether they are
complimentary or not. He reminds me of a very businesslike bird."
Other Americans, referring to the prime minister's changing priorities and his attention to his own domestic political situation, described him more caustically as "a political weather vane" and a
"greased marble spinning on a glass tabletop." To his cabinet, Wilson characterized Lloyd George as a "practical man but no ideal-
ist." Of the president, Lloyd George told a confidant, "I cannot
quite understand him. I am not quite sure whether he is always what
he appears to be in private. He always seems to keep on the mask."

Most of the crucial issues were decided by these three statesmen. They met frequently in secret, leading to criticism by journalists, by representatives of smaller nations, and by their own
countrymen who were excluded from the sessions. Members of
the press accused the president of violating his own principle of
"open covenants of peace, openly arrived at" by conducting such
vital negotiations in private. One British official complained that
they "meet together and think they have decided things, but there
is no one to record what they have done. The consequence is that
misunderstandings often arise and there is no definite account of
their proceedings and nothing happens." Some of the sessions
were acrimonious; early in the conference House described one
meeting where "the President was angry, Lloyd George was angry,
and so was Clemenceau. It is the first time the President has shown
any temper in his dealings with them."

Wilson insisted on personally attending to each detail of the
peace treaty, relying at times on House's assistance but increas-

ingly withdrawing from the rest of the American team. Maps of the world hung on the walls of his hotel rooms, where he frequently met with Clemenceau and Lloyd George. Lansing, who doubted the value of the League and was rarely in Wilson's confidence, wrote that "this personal and clandestine method of negotiation was probably due to the President's belief that he could in this way exercise more effectively his personal influence in favor of the acceptance of the League." Wilson's wife watched him "growing grimmer and graver, day by day" as he continued the "grinding" and "unceasing" work of the treaty. According to Baruch, the president "literally worked himself to the bone and everybody else to a standstill in Paris."

Wilson and the American delegation had prepared to take the high road at Versailles while implementing the Fourteen Points. To Wilson, the major accomplishment of the peace settlement was the successful establishment of the League of Nations; he was also pleased that, in line with his wishes, parts of the map of Europe were redrawn along somewhat more ethnographic lines. Otherwise, Wilson had to compromise on virtually all his principles, especially regarding the severity of the peace imposed on Germany.

The Versailles Treaty included many terms that the Germans widely resented, such as the loss of strategically significant border territories to France, the splitting of East Prussia from the rest of Germany, and the reassignment of Germany's colonies to various Allied countries. The treaty's "war guilt clause" forced the German government to confess its alleged role as the principal aggressor in starting the war. As further humiliations, the Allies were to occupy militarily Germany's industrial heartland for fifteen years, and German military forces were restricted to small constabulary levels. Also created was an Allied reparations commission, which later determined that Germany owed $31 billion in war damages—a completely unrealistic sum for the defeated nation to pay in the near future in view of its destabilized economy.

The American president accepted the harsh provisions against Germany mainly to get French and British support for the terms of the League Covenant and its inclusion in the peace treaties with all the Central powers. Wilson chaired the commission that drafted the Covenant, which generally satisfied the American delegation and with a few revisions was adopted by the plenary session that June. Wilson felt supremely confident that whatever seeds of future discord might have been planted in the Versailles Treaty, "his" League of Nations would adequately guarantee global peace and order in the decades to come. Unfortunately, the League never came close to fulfilling Wilson's expectations, and the harsh penalties against Germany later provided excellent propaganda for Nazi recruiters while failing to deter German rearmament and renewed aggression.

The Council of Three summoned the rest of the Allies and the Germans to accept their final handiwork, which in the end consisted of 440 articles including the German Peace Treaty and the League of Nations Covenant. With great formality, the Treaty of Versailles was signed on June 28, 1919, in the Hall of Mirrors in the palace of Versailles. On the palace grounds after the close of the ceremony, cannons fired, water flowed in the fountains for the first time since the war's start, airplanes flew overhead, and large crowds cheered. House commented that "the affair was elaborately staged and made as humiliating to the enemy as it well could be." The president left for the United States the next day.

By the conclusion of Wilson's work in Europe, Senate approval of the treaty was already in doubt. In mid-February he had returned to the United States for a month to promote the League Covenant, then in draft form. The American public at that time strongly favored participation in the postwar international body, and nearly three-fourths of the state legislatures endorsed the treaty. The membership of the Senate, where the approval of a two-thirds majority was required, was sharply divided. Generally, Democratic senators agreed with the president, while the Republican majority largely opposed the draft Covenant unless major revisions were made.

Prominent among the opponents was a group of isolationist senators from both parties, who called themselves the "Irreconcilables" and rejected any American participation in the League of Nations, regardless of whether its charter was amended. Their leading spokesman was Republican Senator William E. Borah of

Idaho, a fiery orator known for his ability to spellbind audiences. Although he had supported American entry into the war, he vehemently opposed further entanglement in world politics. Borah charged that American membership in the League would transfer "the power to declare war from the Congress of the United States to some tribunal" not controlled by the American people. According to the senator, the League could send American soldiers "to Europe and Asia and Africa whenever any disturbance arises, although it may not affect our people at all." He warned that Americans would be drafted to fill the League's forces, asking: "Would the citizens of the United States volunteer to enter the army for the purpose, for instance, of settling difficulties in the Balkans?"

Also darkening the prospects for Wilson's League campaign on Capitol Hill was the Senate Foreign Relations Committee, which was headed by the formidable leader of the self-styled "reservationists," Senator Lodge of Massachusetts. An annoying rasp in his voice and an often condescending attitude made Lodge a less effective speaker than Borah but did not diminish his power in the Senate. One observer in the gallery described him as "autocratic" and "easily angered," leading "him to sizzle like fat dropping on a hot stove." A former college professor like Wilson, the senator held the Ph.D. in political science (the first such degree granted by Harvard) and was known in Washington as "the scholar in politics" until Wilson's election brought him to town. Among his peers on Capitol Hill, the senator's strong influence was based on his Harvard ties, his considerable wealth and aristocratic standing, and his effective legislative tactics. Adding to his authority was his longtime closeness to Theodore Roosevelt, who dismissed the president's program as "fourteen scraps of paper."

Lodge demanded that a series of "reservations," initially fourteen in number, be added to the treaty before he would support it. Lodge's changes would substantially restrict American participation in the League and would, in the president's view, nullify the treaty. People who knew or studied Lodge differ as to whether his motivation was to protect American sovereignty and self-interests or basically to block American membership in the League. Before the war Lodge had opposed the president's handling of Mexico and neutrality issues, demonstrating clearly his intense distaste for Wilson. By the time of the peace negotiations, the relationship between Wilson and Lodge had become deeply personal and hostile. According to one member of the Wilson administration, "Lodge has one passion—hatred of Wilson." Lodge's principal biographer maintains that during the Senate treaty fight, Lodge "allowed his personal feelings and his partisanship to influence his activities in a most unstatesmanlike way. Considering the enormous importance of the question [of the treaty], he behaved reprehensibly." These words could be equally applied to Wilson; indeed, the argument will continue over which man had more to do with dooming United States membership in the League of Nations, Wilson or Lodge.

In early March 1919, thirty-nine Senate Republicans (including two senators-elect) declared in a public "round-robin" letter that they opposed "Wilson's treaty" without major revision and that the Allies should approve peace treaties with the Central powers before considering any charter for an international organization. While Wilson returned to Paris later that month to complete the rest of the lengthy Versailles Treaty, the Republican-dominated Senate and its Foreign Relations Committee conducted almost interminable hearings on the document, allowing much time to anti-treaty spokesmen.

Meanwhile, well-to-do Republicans, led by Andrew Mellon and Henry Clay Frick, contributed heavily to campaigns advocating the rejection or drastic modification of the Versailles Treaty, especially its League of Nations provisions. By late June, when the treaty was adopted by the thirty-two Allied governments and sullenly accepted by the German delegation, the tide of American public opinion had gradually shifted away from its protreaty leanings. Reservationist and isolationist propaganda, along with spreading war weariness and reluctance to support further international obligations, all contributed to waning prospects for American ratification of the treaty.

In September the Senate Foreign Relations Committee presented forty-five amendments and four reservations to the treaty to the Senate for approval. Lodge's original reservations had grown wildly into such a confused mess that the committee report appeared to call for the treaty's rejection and not simply its revision. The principal reservations would have guaranteed the independence and territorial integrity of the United States and the protection of the Monroe Doctrine, while prohibiting multiple votes for the British Empire and refusing to recognize Japan's seizure of the Shantung Peninsula from hapless China. Some analysts believe that if Wilson had yielded on these four changes, a two-thirds majority might have voted for the treaty. The president instead insisted on a treaty without revision and so urged his Democratic loyalists in the Senate. None of the three main groups in the Senate—reservationists, isolationists, or pro-administration senators—could alone or in combination with members of another faction command the votes to secure passage of a measure expressing their position.

Desperately striving to save his fading treaty support, the president took his case to the people in the hope of pressuring the Senate to carry out his will. Traveling by train, he undertook an extensive speaking tour across the nation on behalf of the unchanged treaty. To his audiences he explained that "the heart of the Covenant is that there shall be no war." He claimed that adding reservations to the treaty was impossible and that "We must take it or leave it." The president characterized opponents of the treaty as "contemptible quitters." His health, which had been weakened by the intense strain of the Paris negotiations, worsened dramatically during his trip. On September 19 in Pueblo, Colorado, he became seriously ill and returned to Washington; a stroke soon left him an invalid and ended his crusade.

The Senate voted twice on the Versailles Treaty on November 19, first rejecting the treaty with Lodge's reservations by a vote of 55-39 and then defeating the treaty in its original form with 53 votes for and 38 against. Although the president could not physically take the lead any longer, a national movement on behalf of the treaty subsequently showed considerable temporary strength through petitions and letters. As a result the Senate agreed to vote a third time on the treaty with reservations. Again, Wilson sent word to his Democratic supporters in the Senate to stand firm for the unchanged treaty. On March 20, 1920, the Wilson loyalists and Borah's Irreconcilables sided with each other and downed the treaty with Lodge's reservations; the vote was 49 for and 35 against. If seven more Democrats had abandoned Wilson's uncompromising position, the necessary two-thirds for passage would have been achieved.

In spite of these votes, Wilson still believed strongly that the American people favored the nation's participation in the League. The president staunchly maintained that the voters should make the presidential election of 1920 "a great and a solemn referendum" on the League. That campaign, however, would not turn out to be a very serious, solemn, or clear mandate on any issue.

By a joint resolution in July 1921, four months after Wilson left office, Congress declared an end to the war with Germany and Austria-Hungary, reserving for the United States all rights secured by the armistice, the Versailles Treaty, or "as a result of the war." That October, separate United States peace treaties were ratified with Germany, Austria, and Hungary. These pacts confirmed that "all the rights and advantages" the Allies had obtained at Paris pertained also to the United States, though America was not obligated to implement or enforce the peace agreements. The United States did not join the League of Nations. Thus a disappointed and frustrated Wilson laid down the mantle of internationalism, which would not be assumed by another American president until Franklin D. Roosevelt.

End of an Era

The years immediately following World War I were characterized in the United States by an increasingly negative attitude. Most of the American people appeared relieved to be free again from war, from Europe's distresses, and from commitments to any major international responsibilities. At home they seemed ready to abandon the progressive reforms that had engendered such excitement since the turn of the century. Political candidates often found favor with the voters if they advocated reducing the size of the federal government and lessening its controls on the growth of affluence.

The nation appeared to be on the threshold of a wild era of rampant materialism that would nearly demolish any lingering ideals of progressivism or internationalism.

It was not unexpected perhaps that such public sentiments would focus first on returning the military establishment to the virtual impotence it had endured during the decades between past American wars. The American armed forces, which had peaked at nearly 4.4 million personnel in late 1918, were cut to 344,000 by 1920. The nine-division U.S. Third Army, which held an occupation zone in the Rhineland centered on Coblenz, remained at its full strength only from December 1918 to June 1919. By the end of that summer the bulk of the American troops had returned to the United States. The remaining American units evacuated the Coblenz zone in early 1923, though the British and French forces stayed in the Rhineland for a considerable time.

By the time Russia withdrew from the World War, it was wracked by civil war. The Allies wanted to send troops there, initially to open a second front against Germany and later to help the White Russian rebels overthrow the Red (Bolshevik) government. They persuaded Wilson that Allied intervention could make a difference, and he reluctantly agreed to send American troops. Like many Americans, Wilson believed that the Bolshevik revolution in Russia and the very nature of Marxism, with its inherent atheism, were anathemas to the interests and values of America and of Western civilization.

In June 1918, a British-led expedition including French and American troops captured the northern Russian port of Murmansk and two months later took Archangel, a Russian port to the south. The Allied forces were never adequately reinforced or resupplied, though they fought several sharp battles against the Red Army, or "Bolos." The American contingent of 5,000 men, known as the "Polar Bears," endured horrible conditions, described in one soldier's diary: "One nerve wracking day, whole platoon lay in snow all night. Don't want any more ordeals like this." The men questioned their mission, especially after the armistice, when their fellow soldiers in France no longer faced enemy fire. One lieutenant summed up the thoughts of many: "What are we doing here anyway? The people won't help themselves. They are nearly all Bolsheviks. If this is not interfering with Russian politics I miss my guess." The president ordered the American soldiers to return home in August 1919; the rest of the Allied forces in that Russian region left two months later. The Bolsheviks had successfully contained the Allied mission, which achieved none of its ill-defined goals.

The president also sent American troops to the eastern part of Russia, where Japan had seized the Russian naval base at Vladivostok. The U.S. force numbered 10,000 and was led by Major General William S. Graves. Arriving by sea in Siberia in July 1918, its specific mission was to rescue a Czech legion of anti-Bolshevik troops fleeing eastward across Russia from the European battlefront. Graves's charge also included the rather impossible objective of discouraging Japanese troops from expanding farther into Russia, with a caveat against becoming entangled in Bolshevik affairs. While the Americans guarded the Trans-Siberian Railway west of Vladivostok, they fought several small engagements against both White and Red Russian soldiers. Thanks mainly to Graves's judicious leadership, the fighting did not escalate, and he managed to avoid clashes with Japanese units, though tensions often ran dangerously high between the Americans and Japanese. After the Reds had suppressed the White Russian revolt and the Czechs had departed safely by sea, Graves's force was evacuated in April 1920. The Japanese, however, would not leave the Russian Far East for another thirty months.

The small-scale American contributions in the Murmansk and Vladivostok regions accomplished little toward destabilizing the Red regime or curbing Japanese imperialism. It was fortunate that neither American contingent was wiped out by the much larger Bolshevik forces; such a catastrophe would have likely led to even greater American interference in Russia or the new Soviet Union (established in 1922). As it was, the two Allied interventions in Russia left a bitter impression on the Russian people and their government. Partly because of these episodes, the United States and the Soviet Union delayed establishing diplomatic relations with each other until 1933.

After withdrawing its military forces from the Rhineland and Russia, the United States maintained only a few small garrisons outside American territories—in China, at Tientsin (and briefly at Shanghai), and in Latin America, notably in Nicaragua, Haiti, and the Dominican Republic. The largest American overseas bases were in the Philippines, Hawaii, Alaska, and the Panama Canal Zone, though none was capable of withstanding a strong enemy assault. Indeed, the garrisons in the West Pacific were so vulnerable that American military planners already considered Japan likely to seize Guam, Wake Island, and the Philippines from the United States.

The American military's experience in the Great War logically led Army and Navy leaders to study what changes needed to be made. These inquiries resulted in the National Defense Act of June 1920, one of the most farsighted and carefully conceived military measures ever passed and ratified by an American Congress and president. At last, the Army high command endorsed the citizen-soldier's worth, ending a long debate about the ability of militia-type forces to achieve high-level combat efficiency. The generally impressive performances of the citizen-soldiers in the First World War led to new emphasis on reserve and militia forces. The measure also provided for a sweeping reorganization of the Army, dividing it into the Regular Army, the National Guard, and the Organized Reserves. The Army's authorized strength was far larger than previously allotted during peacetime.

The National Defense Act also provided for two new branches, the Air Service and the Chemical Warfare Service, which, like the strengthened reserves, would prove crucial in World War II. Unfortunately, the wartime Tank Corps was absorbed by the Infantry, to the chagrin of armored leaders like Patton and Major Adna R. Chafee, who foresaw the enormous potential of large, fast-moving tank units. The act also promoted planning for manpower and economic mobilization during the interwar years.

Overall, the lessons of the First World War woven into the National Defense Act were excellent, but there were flaws. For instance, the military for many years was forced to use stockpiles of undependable weapons and munitions from the 1917–1918 period. The act delayed research and development of new weaponry, with the unfortunate result that soldiers in the early days of the Second World War had to rely on inadequate, obsolete firepower and too many defective shells. Most serious, however, were the external factors that prevented the full implementation of this sound military reorganization plan. In the 1920s, the parsimonious Republican-dominated congresses failed to fund the programs authorized by the 1920 act, and the onset of the Great Depression in the 1930s removed the option of building an adequate military establishment. As a consequence, by the mid-1930s, the U.S. Army ranked seventeenth in size among the armies of the world, well behind even Portugal's.

During the long months of acrimonious maneuvering relating to the peace treaty fight, other manifestations of the immediate postwar negativism gripped America. Economic dislocation, sharp recession, and violent suppression of strikes marred the worlds of factory and mine workers. Trade unionism was sorely handicapped by unfavorable federal court decisions on strike cases. Organized labor, which had enjoyed considerable affluence during the war, now turned against Wilson and the Democrats, and, as in the wake of previous American wars, unemployed veterans added to the clamor for change in Washington.

Increased radicalism, civil unrest, and violence added to the widespread American fear and suspicion over the spread of Bolshevism and precipitated the "Great Red Scare" of late 1918 through mid-1920. Many events contributed to the public's anxiety. In early 1919, a shipyard strike in Seattle escalated into a general strike, which the public associated with revolution and communism. One headline announced: "Reds Directing Seattle Strike—To Test Chance for Revolution." Another newspaper warned, "This is America—Not Russia." In an incident widely believed to be a terrorist act, a horse-drawn wagon parked on New York's Wall Street exploded with such force that it killed thirty-eight people, burned workers in offices six stories above the blast, and blew out windows for blocks. Terrorists mailed bombs to prominent public and business officials and threw bombs at the homes of others, including Attorney General A. Mitchell Palmer.

Under the direction of Palmer, known as the "fighting Quaker," the Department of Justice reacted vigorously. Using legislation passed to control wartime dissent, the government and vigilante groups targeted communist and radical labor organizations in particular. In a spectacular series of raids one day, 4,000 alleged radicals in 23 states were arrested, with many of them subsequently deported to Russia. Palmer claimed that "the 'Reds' were criminal aliens" who had no right to live in the United States. His efforts were directed, he said, to end the "blaze of revolution" which "like a prairie-fire" was "sweeping over every American institution of law and order."

Also building on the suspicion of immigrants was the Ku Klux Klan, which underwent a strong revival from 1915 to 1926 in the South and Midwest. In the prior century it had attracted mostly rural whites by promising to keep African Americans, Roman Catholics, and Jews "in line." Its main recruitment theme during the era of the First World War was nativism, which opposed foreign immigration to America, especially from areas outside Northwest Europe, and harassed the "undesirables" from abroad who were already residents in the United States.

In Washington, the gates of the White House grounds, which had stood open before the war, stayed closed. Within its walls, Wilson remained ill, disillusioned, and isolated. Sadly, House, Lansing, and a number of congressional Democrats who had supported the president in his treaty crusade now found themselves persona non grata at the White House because of their differences with the stricken chief executive. The president had become upset with House as he appeared to bargain too freely with the Allies during the treaty negotiations; when Wilson left France after the signing at Versailles, the two men, once the closest of friends, never met again. The president forced Lansing to resign in early 1920, complaining that the secretary of state had called cabinet meetings while Wilson was ill.

Nationwide, most citizens remained confused or numb over the League or any reform issues; their sympathy for Wilson seemed to decline with his increasing absence from the public scene, however justified. Democratic party leaders looking toward the 1920 presidential election were not optimistic. Although the president endorsed no candidate, each of the three Democratic frontrunners was identified in some way with him or the treaty: Attorney General Palmer of "Red Scare" fame or infamy; former Secretary of the Treasury McAdoo, Wilson's son-in-law; and Governor James M. Cox of Ohio, who had run his state well but was known to support Wilson and the Versailles Treaty. At their national convention in San Francisco, the Democrats needed forty-four ballots to nominate Cox as the presidential candidate. Cox and his vice presidential partner, Franklin D. Roosevelt, wartime assistant secretary of the Navy, bravely defended the Versailles Treaty throughout the campaign, although they probably knew it had become irrelevant to most Americans by then.

The Republican leadership was well aware of the shifting sentiment of the voters toward a more conservative, isolationist position. Progressive Republicans who had broken with their party and backed Wilson in the 1916 presidential race now returned to the regular party fold for the 1920 election. One of the party's best potential candidates was Charles Evans Hughes, the distinguished former Supreme Court justice who had given Wilson a close race in 1916. Hughes, grieving over the death of his daughter, showed no interest in entering the rough-and-tumble turmoil of another presidential campaign. A number of other men sought the nomination, but the convention deadlocked over General Wood and Illinois Governor Frank O. Lowden. On the tenth ballot the convention chose the most acceptable conservative candidate, Senator Warren G. Hard-ing, a former newspaper editor from Ohio with an unremarkable career in the Senate. The vice presidential candidacy went to Governor Calvin Coolidge of Massachusetts, whose sole claim to fame had been his tough declaration regarding a Boston police strike, "There is no right to strike against the public safety, by anybody, anywhere, any time." Having selected inoffensive candidates, the convention adopted a platform that would not split the party over the League issue; it opposed the League Covenant that Wilson had championed but vaguely supported a future "agreement among the nations to preserve the peace of the world."

Supremely confident but not inspired, Harding conducted his campaign from his front porch. He proclaimed that "America's present need is not heroics but healing, not nostrums but normalcy, not revolution but restoration . . . not surgery but serenity." American voters responded to his pledge for a "return to normalcy," and Harding won easily, getting 16.2 million popular votes to Cox's 9.1 million. Receiving 920,000 votes was Eugene Debs, representing the Socialist Labor party while concurrently serving a ten-year prison sentence for supposed sedition during the war. The electoral margin was also a landslide: Harding, 404, and Cox, 127 (all from the South). Normalcy seemed to have triumphed, though actually no substantive issue was explored deeply in the 1920 race. The following November, on the third anniversary of the armistice, President Harding, military representatives from other nations, and crowds of Americans assembled in Arlington National Cemetery for the interment of the Unknown Soldier.

The years of the Wilson administration were characterized by striking contrasts, of which three led to turning points in the history of the United States and perhaps of the world. First, President Wilson in 1913 looked forward to leading his nation to a zenith of progressive reforms in making the political, economic, and social life of America more fair, just, and democratic. He was deeply committed to domestic concerns; diplomatic and military affairs were of far less interest to him. Ironically, international developments played an enormous role in molding the pattern of his presidency. Much of his time was devoted to foreign relations, and his unique form of moral diplomacy led him and the United States to intervene in situations that were of little or no pertinence to American self-interests, especially its security. A high-minded scholar who despised European colonialism, he became one of the chief architects of American political and economic imperialism. A man with a largely negative view of things military, he found himself the commander in chief of the largest military force in the nation's annals and the first major American venture into an overseas war.

Second, the Wilson years comprised a time when the United States achieved the status of a world power in the key areas of economic strength and the pioneering of corporate systems and strategies. But this new global leader in business and international trade,

even then expected to surge far ahead of the major European powers in the postwar age, instead buried its potential for super-power
leadership and turned back to economic nationalism and go-it-
alone trade policies.

Third, though it emerged from the First World War with a
large and respected fighting machine, the United States was quick
to forsake the lessons of the war, largely dismantling its forces and
leaving the field of international security in disarray. America's
unprecedented withdrawal from global responsibility became a
crucial factor in the subsequent emergence of the aggressive, ex-
pansionist regimes of the Axis powers, helping to set the stage,
once again, for a "war to end all wars."

BIBLIOGRAPHICAL ESSAY

Most of the literature on World War I, not surprisingly, is by Europeans. Nevertheless, the number of works on the American aspects of the war and the World War I era has been considerable, especially in recent decades. As in the historiography of other wars, the contemporary trend of American historical interest in the Great War has been toward nonmilitary subjects. On the military side there still has been impressive activity, particularly in directions beyond the traditional battles-and-leaders approach.

Among general works on the First World War, a brilliant, provocative book is Paul Fussell, *The Great War and Modern Memory* (New York, 1975). Useful, especially on historiography, is John M. Cooper, Jr., ed., *Causes and Consequences of World War I* (New York, 1972), which includes several pieces on the United States and the conflict. Contributions by leading scholars like Gordon A. Craig make reading Jack J. Roth, ed., *World War I: A Turning Point in Modern History: Essays on the Significance of the War* (New York, 1967), an enlightening venture.

Of the many one-volume studies of the military side of the war, four stand out for their reasonably balanced perspective on

American achievements: Martin Gilbert, *The First World War: A Complete History* (New York, 1994), an excellent job by the premier British scholar on Churchill; B. H. Liddell Hart, *The Real War, 1914–1918* (Boston, 1930), by the foremost British strategist between the world wars; S. L. A. Marshall, *World War I* (New York, 1985), a valiant effort at objectivity and eloquence by an outspoken, sharp American general; and Allan R. Millett and Williamson Murray, eds., *Military Effectiveness,* vol. 1, *The First World War* (Boston, 1988), an ambitious work edited by two well-known American military historians and including an interesting essay by Timothy K. Nenninger on American effectiveness in the war.

Two very different books on the American military participation, both by highly respected academics, are Edward M. Coffman, *The War to End All Wars: The American Military Experience in World War I* (New York, 1968), still the best single volume on the subject; and Frank Freidel, *Over There: The Story of America's First Great Overseas Crusade,* rev. ed. (New York, 1990), a colorfully written, profusely illustrated work.

A number of period volumes provide excellent, reasonably short surveys, each with challenging theses that are suggested in their titles. The best are those covering the era in Harper and Row's acclaimed New American Nation Series: Arthur S. Link, *Woodrow Wilson and the Progressive Era, 1910–1917* (New York, 1954), by the dean of Wilsonian studies; and Robert H. Ferrell, *Woodrow Wilson and World War I, 1917–1921* (New York, 1985), a versatile scholar's absorbing account. Unchallenged as the top work on the home front is David M. Kennedy, *Over Here: The First World War and American Society* (New York, 1980). For many years the most thorough study and still helpful is Frederic L. Paxson, *American Democracy and the World War* (3 vols., Boston, 1936–1948), which spans 1913–1923, the middle volume being on 1917–1918. A superbly insightful contribution is Henry F. May, *The End of American Innocence: A Study of the First Years of Our Own Time, 1912–1917* (New York, 1959). Ronald Schaffer, *America in the Great War: The Rise of the War Welfare State* (New York, 1991); Ellis W. Hawley, *The Great War and the Search for a Modern Order: A History of the American People and Their Insti-*

tutions, 1917–1933 (New York, 1979); and Daniel M. Smith, *The Great Departure: The United States and World War I, 1914–1920* (New York, 1965), are good surveys, with Smith's book best suited for an American diplomatic history course.

Writings about Wilson, who was surely the most influential American leader in foreign and domestic affairs during the age of the Great War, have been many and contentious, the various schools of opinion differing principally about his success or failure in dealing with the belligerents before the war and in handling the Versailles Treaty issues in Paris and Washington. The published primary collection that is essential for Wilson research is Arthur S. Link, et al., eds., *The Papers of Woodrow Wilson* (69 vols., Princeton, 1966–1994). A much more limited selection is Ray S. Baker and William E. Dodd, eds., *Public Papers of Woodrow Wilson* (6 vols., New York, 1925–1927). The ongoing definitive biography is Arthur S. Link, *Wilson* (5 vols., Princeton, 1947–1965), the most recent volume covering 1916–1917. Arthur C. Walworth won a Pulitzer Prize for his *Woodrow Wilson* (2 vols., New York, 1958). A fresh study that is highly critical and measures Wilson largely in terms of his inconsistent alliance with the American left is Thomas J. Knock, *To End All Wars: Woodrow Wilson and the Quest for a New World Order* (New York, 1992), which won the Warren F. Kuehl Prize of the Society for Historians of American Foreign Relations. Two books by first-rate scholars that compare Wilson with contemporaries in thoughtful ways are Alexander L. George and Juliett L. George, *Woodrow Wilson and Colonel House: A Personality Study* (New York, 1956), and John M. Cooper, Jr., *The Warrior and the Priest: Woodrow Wilson and Theo-dore Roosevelt* (Cambridge, Mass., 1983). Also strongly recommended are two studies whose principal arguments are signaled in their titles: John M. Blum, *Woodrow Wilson and the Politics of Morality* (Boston, 1956), and Edward H. Buehrig, *Woodrow Wilson and the Balance of Power* (Bloomington, Ind., 1955). A solidly researched but still much debated work is Edwin A. Weinstein, *Woodrow Wilson: A Medical and Psychological Biography* (Princeton, 1981). Wilson's final period is approached from other angles in Gene Smith, *When the Cheering Stopped: The Last Years of Woodrow Wilson* (New York, 1964), a serious study but vividly written. Of the numerous reminiscences written by Wilson's colleagues, one of the most insightful is Joseph P. Tumulty, *Woodrow Wilson as I Know Him* (Garden City, N.Y., 1921), by his private secretary from Wilson's New Jersey governorship through his presidency, 1910–1921.

Other significant memoirs by men close to Wilson are Edward M. House, *The Intimate Papers of Colonel House,* ed. Charles Seymour (4 vols., Boston, 1926–1928), rich insights by the president's chief confidant; Robert Lansing, *The War Memoirs of Robert Lansing, Secretary of State* (Indianapolis, Ind., 1935), by the secretary of state who, like House, lost Wilson's trust in 1919; William G. McAdoo, *Crowded Years: The Reminiscences of William G. McAdoo* (Boston, 1931), by the president's son-in-law and holder of several important administration posts; and Ray S. Baker, *American Chronicle: The Autobiography of Ray Stannard Baker* (New York, 1945), who also produced at least sixteen other volumes dealing with the Wilson presidency. Two superb biographies of Wilson lieutenants are John M. Blum, *Joe Tumulty and the Wilson Era* (Boston, 1951), on the presidential secretary's world; and John M. Cooper, Jr., *Walter Hines Page: The Southerner as American, 1855–1918* (Chapel Hill, N.C., 1977), about the influential ambassador to St. James's Court.

Diplomacy during the Wilson administration has attracted the attention of a host of good historians, among the most noteworthy works being two on the United States and Mexico: Robert E. Quirk, *An Affair of Honor: Woodrow Wilson and the Occupation of Veracruz* (Lexington, Ky., 1962), a fascinating study; and Mark T. Gilderhus, *Diplomacy and Revolution: U.S.-Mexican Relations Under Wilson and Carranza* (Tucson, 1977), a perceptive critique of much-flawed policies by both sides. Of the considerable amount of writing on U.S.–East Asian policy during the period, two of the soundest monographs are Burton F. Beers, *Vain Endeavor: Robert Lansing's Attempts to End the American-Japanese Rivalry* (Durham, N.C., 1962), and Russell H. Fifield, *Woodrow Wilson and the Far East: The Diplomacy of the Shantung Question* (New York, 1952).

The tortuous road to war in Europe for the United States, 1914–1917, has generated a huge amount of contentious writing. Some of the outstanding books on America's entry into the war are Ernest R. May, *The World War and American Isolation, 1914–1917* (Cambridge, Mass., 1959), which lucidly links the issue of U.S. intervention to changes in German internal and foreign policies; Daniel M. Smith, *Robert Lansing and American Neutrality, 1914–1917* (New York, 1972), an excellent study of a secretary of state with many liabilities in a time of great crises; John M. Cooper, Jr., *The Vanity of Power: American Isolationism and the First World War, 1914–1917* (Westport, Conn., 1969), an in-depth look at the impact of isolationist influence during the prewar period; and Frederick S. Calhoun, *Power and Principle: Armed Intervention in Wilsonian Foreign Policy* (Kent, Ohio, 1986), and Warren I. Cohen, *The American Revisionists: The Lessons of Intervention in World War I* (Chicago, 1967), both well-researched and thoughtful. Older works that still deserve attention are Charles Seymour, *American Diplomacy During the World War* (Baltimore, 1942), first published in 1934; and Benedict Crowell and Robert F. Wilson, *How America Went to War* (6 vols., New Haven, Conn., 1921). On the European background of the Great War, see James Joll, *The Origins of the First World War* (London, 1992), which first came out in 1984; and Laurence Lafore, *The Long Fuse: An Interpretation of the Origins of World War I* (Philadelphia, 1965), which attracted widespread attention.

The most thorough coverage of the naval war in general is Thomas G. Frothingham, *The Naval History of the World War* (3 vols., Cambridge, Mass., 1924–1926), which has a strongly British focus. The most recent and balanced works have been by Americans: Paul G. Halpern, *A Naval History of World War I* (Annapolis, Md., 1994), a solid, detailed account; and Paolo Coletta, *Allied and American Naval Operations in the European Theater, World War I* (Lewiston, N.Y., 1996), an important contribution by an esteemed naval historian. An excellent study on politics, policies, and strategy-making is David F. Trask, *Captains and Cabinets: Anglo-American Naval Relations, 1917–1918* (Columbia, Mo., 1972), by a former U.S. Army and State Department historian.

The two foremost American naval leaders of the war, the heads of the Navy Department and of U.S. forces in European waters, have solid studies by and about them. The wartime secretary of the Navy published *The Cabinet Diaries of Josephus Daniels, 1913–1921* (Lincoln, Neb., 1963); and, in turn, Joseph L. Morrison, *Josephus Daniels* (Chapel Hill, N.C., 1967) is a commendable work about the man and his long career in journalism and diplomacy as well as with the Navy. A vividly written memoir is William S. Sims and Burton J. Hendrick, *Victory at Sea* (Garden City, N.Y., 1920), covering Admiral Sims's wartime experience; the outspoken but very able admiral is the subject of a fine biography in Elting E. Morison, *Admiral Sims and the Modern American Navy* (Boston, 1942).

The basic official documents relating to the AEF are found in U.S. Department of the Army, Office of the Chief of Military History, *United States Army in the World War, 1917–1919* (17 vols., Washington, 1948); and U.S. Department of the Army, Office of the Chief of Military History, *Order of Battle of the United States Land Forces in the World War* (5 vols., Washington, 1931–1949).

A trustworthy companion for tourists of the American battle sites or even for an advanced student of the AEF is American Battle Monuments Commission, *American Armies and Battlefields in Europe: A History, Guide, and Reference Book* (Washington, 1962), which the Army first issued in 1938. Another general work on the AEF but one intended to make readers rethink the strategy and grand tactics of the Allied senior leaders is David F. Trask, *The AEF and Coalition Warmaking, 1917–1918* (Lawrence, Kans., 1993), the focus being on the St. Mihiel and Meuse-Argonne campaigns and Pershing's near-disastrous decisions and planning at critical times. On the life of the soldiers, Laurence Stallings, *The Doughboys: The Story of the AEF, 1917–1918* (New York, 1963), is already attaining near-classic status; John Ellis, *Eye-Deep in Hell: Trench Warfare in World War I* (New York, 1976), is a moving account by the premier chronicler of GI life in World War II as well; and Fred D. Baldwin, "The American Enlisted Man in World War I" (unpublished Ph.D. dissertation, Princeton University, 1964), is a treasure trove of anecdotes, statistics, and sharp profiles of the doughboys in the United States and abroad.

The best of the autobiographical works by American senior officers are John J. Pershing, *My Experiences in the World War* (2 vols., New York, 1931), which is so critical of the War Department that it prompted an equally biting commentary on AEF leadership by the Army's chief of staff, Peyton C. March, *The Nation at War* (Garden City, 1932). Also, see Hunter Liggett, *Commanding an American Army* (Boston, 1925), by the commander of the U.S. First Army in France; James G. Harbord, *The American Army in France, 1917–1919* (Boston, 1936), the memoirs of the AEF chief of staff and later its supply chief; George C. Marshall, *Memoirs of My Services in the World War, 1917–1918,* ed. James L. Collins, Jr. (Boston, 1976), a belatedly discovered gem by the great Army chief of staff during the Second World War; and D. Clayton James, *The Years of MacArthur,* vol. I (Boston, 1970), which covers MacArthur's life from 1880 to 1941, including his role in World War I.

The choicest works about key Army figures of the war are the two magisterial biographies of the AEF commander: Donald Smythe, *Pershing: General of the Armies* (Bloomington, Ind., 1986), by a Jesuit who also became an expert on the Great War; and Frank E. Vandiver, *Black Jack: The Life and Times of John J. Pershing* (2 vols., College Station, Tex., 1977), by a renowned Civil War scholar and university president. Other significant biographies, all by eminent senior military historians, include Edward M. Coffman, *The Hilt of the Sword: The Career of Peyton C. March* (Madison, Wis., 1966), a fair, solid treatment of the wartime chief of staff; Daniel R. Beaver, *Newton D. Baker and the American War Effort, 1917–1919* (Lincoln, Neb., 1966), a sound work on the secretary of war and progressive reformer; and Allan R. Millett, *The General: Robert L. Bullard and Officership in the United States Army, 1881–1925* (Westport, Conn., 1975), an excellent biography of the commander of the AEF's Second Army. Also noteworthy is a moving account of the AEF's most famous combat hero: David D. Lee, *Sergeant York: An American Hero* (Lexington, Ky., 1985).

Of the two principal campaigns of the AEF, highly recommended are Paul F. Braim, *The Test of Battle: The American Expeditionary Forces in the Meuse-Argonne Campaign* (Newark, N.J.,

1987), the latest examination of the largest U.S. operation to that time; and Frederick Palmer, *Our Greatest Battle (The Meuse-Argonne)* (New York, 1919), the first major look at that campaign and still one of the best. The most recent and finest of the studies of the AEF's first major independent operation is James H. Hallas, *Squandered Victory: the American First Army at St. Mihiel* (Westport, Conn., 1995).

Surely one of the most colorful aspects of World War I for American readers has been the AEF Air Service. The claimant to the position as the newest and best on the subject is James J. Cooke, *The U.S. Air Service in the Great War: 1917–1919* (Westport, Conn., 1996), which should hold the top rung for a long while. By far, the finest biography of the AEF air arm's leader is Alfred F. Hurley, *Billy Mitchell: Crusader for Air Power* (New York, 1964), by an Air Force general, university chancellor, and respected historian. Generally esteemed as definitive on its subject is I. B. Holley, Jr., *Ideas and Weapons: Exploitation of the Aerial Weapons by the United States in World War I* (New Haven, Conn., 1953). Another respected work on AEF air operations is James J. Hudson, *Hostile Skies: A Combat History of the American Air Service in World War I* (Syracuse, N.Y., 1968), while an essential starting place on the AEF Air Service documents is Maurer Maurer, ed. and comp., *The U.S. Air Service in World War I* (4 vols., Washington, 1978–1979). A useful book that affords a broader context is John H. Morrow, Jr., *The Great War in the Air: Military Aviation from 1909–1921* (Washington, 1993).

The enormous literature on the operations of the Allies and Central powers cannot be incorporated in this essay, but the following on the Allied high command and Anglo-American relations are especially pertinent to the context of the American involvement: Correlli Barnett, *The Swordbearers: Supreme Command in the First World War* (New York, 1964), a classic critique of Moltke, Jellicoe, Pétain, and Ludendorff; David F. Trask, *The United States in the Supreme War Council: American War Aims and Inter-Allied Strategy, 1917–1918* (Middletown, Conn., 1961), illuminating on the vital role of Bliss and other American officials in Allied strategy formulation; David R. Woodward, *Trial by*

Friendship: Anglo-American Relations, 1917–1918 (Lexington, Ky., 1993), an outstanding recent monograph with ramifications for the two nations' future wartime ties; Lloyd C. Gardner, *Safe for Democracy: The Anglo-American Response to Revolution, 1913– 1923* (New York, 1984), a perceptive, critical analysis; and Kathleen Burk, *Britain, America, and the Sinews of War, 1914–1918* (Boston, 1985), a study of the logistical links vital to both nations throughout the war.

Loyalty and civil liberties generated excitement during the Wilson period and resulted in many consequent scholarly writings. Standard works on the Creel Committee are Stephen Vaughn, *Holding Fast the Inner Lines: Democracy, Nationalism, and the Committee on Public Information* (Chapel Hill, N.C., 1980), and James R. Mock and Cedric Larson, *Words That Won the War: The Story of the Committee on Public Information* (Princeton, 1939). A brilliant look at higher education's not so admirable role in the Creel era is Carol S. Gruber, *Mars and Minerva: World War I and the Uses of the Higher Learning in America* (Baton Rouge, La., 1975). Other highly regarded studies on their specific topics are Robert K. Murray, *Red Scare: A Study in National Hysteria* (Minneapolis, Minn., 1955); Horace C. Peterson and Gilbert C. Fite, *Opponents of War, 1917–1918* (Madison, Wis., 1957); Stephen M. Kohn, *American Political Prisoners: Prosecutions Under the Espionage and Sedition Acts* (Westport, Conn., 1994); and Frederick C. Luebke, *Bonds of Loyalty: German-Americans and World War I* (Dekalb, Ill., 1974). The best overall work on the federal approach to civil rights at the time is Harry N. Scheiber, *The Wilson Administration and Civil Liberties, 1917–1921* (Ithaca, N.Y., 1960), and Wilson's overly zealous attorney general is candidly analyzed in Stanley Coben, *A. Mitchell Palmer: Politician* (New York, 1963).

The fate of domestic reform efforts and progressives' impact on America's international relations in the Wilson period are traced in Robert D. Johnson, *The Peace Progressives and American Foreign Relations* (Cambridge, Mass., 1995). Two of the most significant works on the evolution of the prohibition amendment are K. Austin Kerr, *Organized for Prohibition: A New History of the Anti-Saloon League* (New Haven, Conn., 1985), and Norman

H. Clark, *Deliver Us from Evil: An Interpretation of American Prohibition* (New York, 1976). Of the many biographies of progressive leaders of the time, one of the finest is John Braeman, *Albert J. Beveridge: American Nationalist* (Chicago, 1971).

Highly commendable studies of women's wartime activities are appearing with growing frequency, three of the most significant and recent being Dorothy Schneider and Carl J. Schneider, *Into the Breach: American Women Overseas in World War I* (New York, 1991); Carrie Foster, *The Women and the Warriors: The United States Section of the Women's International League for Peace and Freedom, 1915–1946* (Syracuse, N.Y., 1995); and Maurine Weiner Greenwald, *Women, War, and Work: The Impact of World War I on Women Workers in the United States* (Westport, Conn., 1980). Good biographies include Jacqueline Van Voris, *Carrie Chapman Catt: A Public Life* (New York, 1987); and Inez Haynes Irwin, *Alice Paul and the Story of the National Woman's Party* (Fairfax, Va., 1977), reprint of a 1921 work with an altered title.

The few triumphs and many tribulations of African Americans are traced in John Hope Franklin, *From Slavery to Freedom: A History of African Americans* (7th ed., New York, 1994), long regarded as the place to begin, especially for the general context. An important study of a far-reaching phenomenon is Florette Henri, *Black Migration: Movement North, 1900–1920* (New York, 1975). A recent book that garnered Pulitzer, Bancroft, and Parkman prizes is David L. Lewis, *W. E. B. Du Bois—Biography of a Race, 1868–1919* (New York, 1993). The problems that blacks faced in the military are accorded balanced treatment in Bernard C. Nalty, *Strength for the Fight: A History of Black Americans in the Military* (New York, 1986); and Arthur E. Barbeau and Florette Henri, *The Unknown Soldiers: Black American Troops in World War I* (Philadelphia, 1974). For the relevant primary materials, see Bernard Nalty and Morris J. MacGregor, *Blacks in the United States Armed Forces: Basic Documents,* vol. 4, *Segregation Entrenched, 1917–1940* (Wilmington, Del., 1977).

There were several major facets to manpower mobilization, including peacetime preparedness, conscription, and organized labor. On the first topic, the main writings include John P. Finnegan,

Against the Specter of a Dragon: The Campaign for American Military Preparedness, 1914–1917 (Westport, Conn., 1974); and John G. Clifford, *The Citizen Soldiers: The Plattsburg Training Camp Movement, 1913–1920* (Lexington, Ky., 1972). An excellent monograph on the draft is John W. Chambers II, *To Raise an Army: The Draft Comes to Modern America* (New York, 1987). For the contributions of two generals who were central to manpower planning, see these two solid studies: I. B. Holley, Jr., *General John M. Palmer, Citizen Soldiers, and the Army of a Democracy* (Westport, Conn., 1982); and David A. Lockmiller, *Enoch H. Crowder: Soldier, Lawyer, and Statesman* (Columbia, Mo., 1955). Trade unionism is ably covered from the federal and labor perspectives in Valerie Jean Conner, *The National War Labor Board: Stability, Social Justice, and the Voluntary State in World War I* (Chapel Hill, N.C., 1983); and Simeon Larson, *Labor and Foreign Policy: Gompers, the AFL, and the First World War, 1914–1918* (Rutherford, N.J., 1974).

Well-regarded works dealing with economic mobilization are William J. Breen, *Uncle Sam at Home: Civilian Mobilization, Wartime Federalism, and the Council of National Defense* (Westport, Conn., 1984); Charles Gilbert, *American Financing of World War I* (Westport, Conn., 1970); and Robert D. Cuff, *The War Industries Board: Business-Government Relations during World War I* (Baltimore, Md., 1973). See also Bernard Baruch, *Baruch: The Public Years* (New York, 1960), the best of his several reminiscences; and War Industries Board, *American Industry in the War* (New York, 1941), which was largely written by the WIB's head, Baruch. The principal work on Baruch is Margaret L. Coit, *Mr. Baruch* (Boston, 1957). On the contributions of the Food Administration and its distinguished leader, see Lawrence E. Gelfand, ed., *Herbert Hoover: The Great War and Its Aftermath, 1914–1923* (Iowa City, Ia., 1979); Herbert Hoover, *America's First Crusade* (New York, 1942); and William C. Mullendore, *History of the United States Food Administration: 1917–1919* (Stanford, Calif., 1941). A solid analysis of the federal role in export-import activities during the Wilson years is Burton I. Kaufman, *Efficiency and Expansion: Foreign Trade Organization in the Wilson Administration, 1913–1921* (Westport, Conn., 1974). To study more about some of the milestone changes in business in the United States, a standard work is Alfred D. Chandler, Jr., *The Visible Hand: The Managerial Revolution in American Business* (Cambridge, Mass., 1977).

An outstanding work on the ending of the hostilities is Harry R. Rudin, *Armistice: 1918* (New Haven, Conn., 1944). Most of the writings relating to the Paris Peace Conference naturally are by European individuals or their governments. Much of the American diplomatic record is found in U.S. Department of State, *Foreign Relations of the United States, 1919: The Paris Peace Conference* (13 vols., Washington, 1942–1947). Also see Harold W. Temperley, ed., *A History of the Peace Conference of Paris* (6 vols., London, 1920–1924). A penetrating evaluation of Wilson's large advisory group of experts at Paris is in Lawrence E. Gelfand, *The Inquiry: American Preparations for Peace, 1917–1919* (New Haven, Conn., 1963). The views and activities of the president's principal consultants are well covered in Inga Floto, *Colonel House in Paris: A Study of American Policy at the Paris Peace Conference, 1919* (Princeton, N.J., 1980); and Robert Lansing, *The Peace Negotiations: A Personal Narrative* (Boston, 1921). For good insights and sound research, three works are strongly recommended: Charles L. Mee, Jr., *The End of Order: Versailles, 1919* (New York, 1980); Arthur C. Walworth, *Wilson and His Peacemakers: American Diplomacy at the Paris Peace Conference, 1919* (New York, 1986); and Klaus Schwabe, *Woodrow Wilson, Revolutionary Germany, and Peacemaking, 1918–1919: Missionary Diplomacy and the Realities of Power* (Chapel Hill, N.C., 1985).

The fight in America over the Versailles Treaty is well covered in Lloyd E. Ambrosius, *Woodrow Wilson and the American Diplomatic Tradition: The Treaty Fight in Perspective* (New York, 1987); Thomas A. Bailey, *Woodrow Wilson and the Lost Peace* (New York, 1945); and Denna F. Fleming, *The United States and the League of Nations, 1918–1920* (New York, 1932), all by historians of distinction whose views differ widely. Lodge and his Reservationists are thoroughly evaluated in William C. Widenor, *Henry Cabot Lodge and the Search for an American Foreign*

Policy (Berkeley, Calif., 1980); and John A. Garraty, *Henry Cabot Lodge: A Biography* (New York, 1968). Borah and his isolationist faction receive sound treatment in Robert J. Maddox, *William E. Borah and American Foreign Policy* (Baton Rouge, La., 1969); and Ralph Stone, *The Irreconcilables: The Fight Against the League of Nations* (Lexington, Ky., 1970).

The unique expeditions of American ground forces in the years 1919–1923 have been surprisingly well covered by scholars. On the American occupation zone in the Rhineland, a dependable account is Keith L. Nelson, *Victors Divided: America and the Allies in Germany, 1918–1923* (Berkeley, Calif., 1975). Outstanding treatises on American-Russian ties from the Bolshevik Revolution to the early 1920s, largely nonmilitary, are George F. Kennan, *Soviet-American Relations, 1917–1920* (Princeton, N.J., 1956–1958), a classic; and two recent contributions with different approaches—David W. McFadden, *Alternative Paths: Soviets and Americans, 1917–1920* (New York, 1993); and Georg Schild, *Between Ideology and Realpolitik: Woodrow Wilson and the Russian Revolution, 1917–1921* (Westport, Conn., 1995). The standard works on the military interventions in Russia are Betty M. Unterberger, *America's Siberian Expedition, 1918–1920: A Study of National Policy* (Durham, N.C., 1956); and J. F. N. Bradley, *Allied Intervention in Russia, 1917–1920* (New York, 1968).

On the turbulent period of postwar economic dislocation and social readjustment, there are an increasing number of scholarly works, along with some old yet useful studies. Among the best of these are Burl Noggle, *Into the Twenties: The United States from Armistice to Normalcy* (Urbana, Ill., 1974); Dixon Wecter, *When Johnny Comes Marching Home* (Boston, 1944); and Melvyn P. Leffler, *The Elusive Quest: America's Pursuit of European Stability and French Security, 1919–1933* (Chapel Hill, N.C., 1979), all by distinguished historians.

The politics of the American scene, 1916–1920, receives excellent coverage in Seward W. Livermore, *Politics is Adjourned: Woodrow Wilson and the War Congress, 1916–1918* (Middletown, Conn., 1966); and Wesley M. Bagby, *The Road to Normalcy: The Presidential Campaign and Election of 1920* (Baltimore, Md., 1962).

The concluding references constitute a variegated group of items that will be helpful to those who are undertaking initial research forays into the area. First, the multiple annual volumes of the U.S. Department of State's marvelous series, *Foreign Relations of the United States* for the years 1913–1921, seem to include a lot of documents, but actually constitute a carefully selected sampling of the most significant papers. A splendid new tool is Anne Cipriano Venzon, ed., *The United States in the First World War: An Encyclopedia* (Hamden, Conn., 1995). Refer also to Holger H. Herwig and Neil M. Heyman, *Biographical Dictionary of World War I* (Westport, Conn., 1982), which is excellent but heavily stresses European figures. Another useful work is Gerald Herman, *The Pivotal Conflict: A Comprehensive Chronology of the First World War, 1914–1919* (New York, 1992). The two principal atlases, both well done, are Martin Gilbert, *Atlas of World War I* (2nd ed., New York, 1994); and Anthony Livesey with H. P. Willmott, *The Historical Atlas of World War I* (New York, 1994). Finally, three bibliographies are recommended: A. G. S. Enser, *A Subject Bibliography of the First World War: Books in English, 1914–1987* (Aldershot, England, 1990), the newest and largest of the group; David R. Woodward and Robert F. Maddox, *America and World War I: A Selected Annotated Bibliography of English-language Sources* (New York, 1985), the sharpest in selectivity and the only one with annotations; and Ronald Schaffer, *The United States in World War I: A Selected Bibliography* (Santa Barbara, Calif., 1978), good but also the oldest and shortest.

INDEX

African Americans
  lynching of, 68
  in military, 57–58
  race relations, 68–69
  rural to urban migration of, 69
  in workforce, 68
Aisne offensive (German), 40–42
Aisne-Marne offensive (Allied), 42
Allied powers
  economic ties with U.S., 13–14
  identification of, 2
  interpretation of fall of Central
    powers, 80–81
  propaganda of, 11–13
  U.S. loans to, 14
Allied reparations commission,
  creation of, 85
Allied Supreme War Council, 5, 39
Alsace, France, stationing of American
  forces in, 36, 52
American Expeditionary Forces
  (AEF), 35–48, 51–58
  casualties, 47–48, 55–56
  German opinion of, 55–56
  under Pershing, 35–38, 44–45
  return of, to U.S., 55, 91
American Federation of Labor (AFL),
  60, 66
American Library Association, 70

Archangel, Russia, Allied capture of, 91
Argonne Forest, France, 44
armistice on Western Front, 47, 48
arms trafficking, between U.S. and
  Allied powers, 13–15
Atlantic cable traffic, British control
  of, 13
Australia, as Allied power, 2
Austria-Hungary
  as Central power, 2
  fall of northeast Italy to, 28
  peace treaty with United States, 90
  ultimatum to Serbia, 1
  will to fight, 29

Baker, Newton D., 49, 56
  attitude of, toward conscientious
    objectors, 34–35
  relationship with Pershing, 35, 56
  as secretary of war, 31–33, 49, 56,
    60, 73, 75
Baruch, Bernard M., 60–62, 85
Beatty, David, 30
Belgium
  as Allied power, 2, 44
  entrance into World War I, 2
  German invasion of, 2, 6, 12
Belleau Wood, battle of, 41–42, 56
  aerial support at, 38

114   INDEX

Eastern Front, 2, 8, 28
Eighteenth Amendment, 76
elections
    of 1912, 22
    of 1916, 22–23, 96
    of 1918, 76–77, 78, 81
    of 1920, 96–97
English as official language movement,
    72
Espionage Act (1917), 71, 72

Fairbanks, Douglas, 65
films, 73–74
Flagg, James Montgomery, 73
"Flying Circus" Squadron, 39
Foch, Ferdinand, 39–40, 42, 43, 45, 47
Food Administration, 62–64, 73
Ford, Henry, 22
Fosdick, Raymond, 49, 54
"Four Minute Men," 73
Fourteen Points, 79–81, 82–83
France
    economic ties with U.S., 14
    entrance into war, 1–2
    intervention in Russia, 91–92
    military operations, 2, 6–9, 28, 39–
        44, 46
    Paris Peace Conference, 83–86
    Pershing, arrival in, 35–36
    postwar occupation of Germany, 91
    relationship with American
        Expeditionary Forces, 36–37,
        52–54
    U.S. attitudes toward, 3
    Wilson, arrival in, 82
Frick, Henry Clay, 88
Fuel Administration, 62

Gallipoli assault (Allied), 2, 7–8
German Americans, 3, 13, 23, 70
Germany
    British naval blockade of, 9–10, 13–
        14, 29, 30
    as Central power, 2
    decision to risk war with U.S., 23–27

entrance into World War I, 1–2
    interest in Fourteen Points, 80
    invasion of Belgium, 2, 6, 12
    Japanese seizure of Pacific and
        Asian holdings, 16–17
    military operations (1914–1917), 6,
        7–9, 28
    military operations (1918), 39–47
    peace treaty with U.S., 90
    postwar occupation of, 48, 85, 91
    sabotage in U.S., 13
    U-boat warfare of, 9–12, 24–25, 26,
        27, 28
    and Versailles Treaty, 85–86, 88
    and Zimmermann telegram, 25–26
    U.S. soldiers, opinion of, 55–56
    U.S. attitudes toward, 3, 11–13, 72–
        74
Gompers, Samuel, 60, 66
Graves, William S., 92
Great Britain
    control of Atlantic cable traffic, 13
    economic ties to U.S., 13–14
    entrance into World War I, 2
    intervention in Russia, 91–92
    military operations (ground), 2, 6–9,
        28, 39–40, 42–43, 44
    naval blockade of, 9–10, 13–14, 29,
        39
    and Paris Peace Conference, 83–86
    postwar occupation of Germany, 91
    propaganda, 11–13
    relationship with American
        Expeditionary Forces, 36–37, 52–
        53
    Zimmermann telegram, interception
        of, 25
Greece, as Allied power, 2
Griffith, D. W., 74
Guantanamo Bay, U.S. naval station at,
    17

Haig, Douglas, 8, 35, 40
Haiti, U.S. intervention in, 17
Harbord, James G., 37

America and the Great War, 1914–1920

Developmental and Copy editor: Andrew J. Davidson
Production Editor: Lucy Herz
Proofreader: Claudia Siler
Indexer: Sandi Schroeder
Cartographer: Jane Domier
Printer: McNaughton & Gunn, Inc.